The Smashing Book

Imprint

Published 2009 by Smashing Media GmbH, Lübeck, Germany.
5th Edition March 2012.
Layout and printing by Sernas Zurzolo & DE Druck Europa GmbH, Germany.
This book was written by Alessandro Cattaneo, Andrew Maier, Chris Spooner,
Darius A Monsef, David Leggett, Dmitry Fadeyev, Jacob Gube, Kayla Knight, Rene Schmidt,
Steven Snell and Jon Tan.

Book cover design: Brian Nelson. The "Rainbow Cat": Min Tran. Illustrations: Dmitry Tsozik,
Anna Myagkova, Anton Zykin. Proofreading: Andrew Lobo. Sales Organization: Michael Dobler.
Concept, editing and idea: Sven Lennartz, Vitaly Friedman and the readers of Smashing Magazine.

Table of Contents

Preface

One can make simple things difficult, and writing a book the normal way just wasn't a challenge enough for us. The list of contributors to the left testifies to that. We wanted to engage as many people as possible: writers, designers, illustrators, editors. In fact, internally, we called this little project "The Community Book". Nevertheless, the book was written not by our readers but by a professional team of authors. And throughout the whole process (from brainstorming to writing to putting the final touches on the layout) we included our audience in our plans: we queried people in the Smashing Forum, collected suggestions and listened to your opinions. Of course, all of this ado in advance was meant to stimulate your appetite, too. The result is what now sits in your hands, Smashing Magazine's first book. We hope we did at least some things in it right.

The book contains no lists of links or aggregated content. It has 10 carefully prepared, written and edited stories that are based upon topic suggestions and wishes of Smashing Magazine's readers. We consider the topics covered here fundamental and so the content is, we hope, highly practical. You can find a list of all of the references and resources mentioned in this book in a handy overview online at *http://smashing-links.com*

Please let us know what you think of the book in your reviews or in comments. Have fun and a truly smashing experience with the Smashing Book, folks!

Sven Lennartz and Vitaly Friedman

Dmitry Fadeyev

User Interface Design in Modern

Web Applications

W hat is user interface design? What makes a user interface effective, and, more importantly, how do you go about crafting a good user interface? This chapter looks at the theory as well as the practical techniques involved in visual interface design in modern Web applications.

What Is A User Interface?

"The way that you accomplish tasks with a product – what you do and how it responds – that's the interface" — *Jef Raskin*

User interface design isn't just about buttons and menus; it's about the interaction between the user and the application or device, and in many cases, it's about the interaction between multiple users through that device. This means that user interface design isn't about how a product looks, but rather about how it works. It's not just about arranging buttons and picking colors, but rather about choosing the right tools for the job. Does a particular interface even need buttons? If so, what do those buttons need to do? What do I need to provide users with so that they can figure out how my application works and accomplish what they want to do with ease?

Even if someone uses an interface for the first time, certain elements can still be familiar.

Working on the user interface early on in the product development life cycle is vital because, as Jef Raskin succinctly puts it, "As far as the customer is concerned, the interface is the product[1]". The user sees and interacts with the user interface, not the underlying back-end architecture of your application. Getting this element right will thus have a big impact on how much your customers enjoy using your product and how easy your product is to use. Start by designing the interface first and then coding the back-end engine that powers it, rather than building the back-end first and then putting an interface "wrapper" over top.

1 Raskin, J., 2000 The Humane Interface Addison Wesley

What Makes A Great User Interface?

Before we proceed to build a user interface for our product, it's important to first understand what makes a good user interface; what are the qualities we should aim to achieve? All great interfaces share eight qualities or characteristics:

1. **Clarity.** The interface avoids ambiguity by making everything clear through language, flow, hierarchy and metaphors for visual elements. Clear interfaces don't need manuals. They also ensure users make less mistakes while using them.

2. **Concision.** It's easy to make the interface clear by over-clarifying and labeling everything, but this leads to interface bloat, where there is just too much stuff on the screen at the same time. If too many things are on the screen, finding what you're looking for is difficult, and so the interface becomes tedious to use. The real challenge in making a great interface is to make it concise and clear at the same time.

3. **Familiarity.** Something is familiar when you recall a previous encounter you've had with it. Even if someone uses an interface for the first time, certain elements can still be familiar. You can use real-life metaphors to communicate meaning; for example, folder-style tabs are often used for navigation on websites and in applications. People recognize them as navigation items because the metaphor of the folder is familiar to them.

4. **Responsiveness.** This means a couple of things. First, responsiveness means speed: a good interface should not feel sluggish. Secondly, the interface should provide good feedback to the user about what's happening and whether the user's input is being successfully processed.

5. **Consistency.** Keeping your interface consistent across your application is important because it allows users to recognize usage patterns. Once your users learn how certain parts of the interface work, they can apply this knowledge to new areas and features, provided that the user interface there is consistent with what they already know.

6. **Aesthetics.** While you don't need to make an interface attractive for it to do its job, making something look good will make the time your users spend using your application more enjoyable; and happier users can only be a good thing.

7. **Efficiency.** Time is money, and a great interface should make the user more productive through shortcuts and good design. After all, this is one of the core benefits of technology: it allows us to perform tasks with less time and effort by doing most of the work for us.

8. **Forgiveness.** Everyone makes mistakes, and how your application handles those mistakes will be a test of its overall quality. Is it easy to undo actions? Is it easy to recover deleted files? A good interface should not punish users for their mistakes but should instead provide the means to remedy them.

Designing a user interface that incorporates all of these characteristics is tricky because working on one characteristic often affects others. The more interface elements you add, the more stuff your users will have to process. Of course, the converse is also true: not providing enough help and support may make certain functions ambiguous. Creating something that is simple and elegant and at the same time clear and consistent is the difficult goal of a user interface designer.

Visual Interface Design Toolbox

Visual interface design is the process of designing the physical representation of your interface as your users would see it on the screen of their electronic device. The objective of visual interface design is to communicate meaning, which is done by crafting appropriate visuals that best represent what the application does and how it can be operated. Creating the look and feel of a product is not the primary aim of visual interface design, merely a component. The primary aim is communication: communicating behavior to help your users understand how your application works.

A number of core elements make up visual interface design. Selecting appropriate types, calibrating each element and then combining them all in a meaningful way let us convey meaning for all the different functions and features of our user interface.

Here are the main building blocks of visual interface design:

Layout and Positioning
Layout provides structure to all the visual elements in your interface. It also defines hierarchy and relationships through the spacing between elements. Bringing elements closer together indicates a relationship between them; for example, labels under icons. Positioning can improve flow, too. For example, positioning labels in forms above text fields, rather than to the left, allows us to move our eyes down them easily, rather than have to keep looking left to check which label applies to which field.

Shape and Size
Shape can be used to differentiate elements; for example, by varying the silhouettes of icons to make them easier and quicker to recognize. Size can be used to indicate importance, bigger elements being more significant. Size can also make clickable controls more usable; Fitt's law tells us that the bigger a clickable area is, the quicker users can move

> Creating the look and feel of a product is not the primary aim of visual interface design, merely a component.

their mouse cursor over it. Making the most frequently used controls bigger will make it easier for your users to click on them, and thus improve the efficiency of the interface.

Color
Color is useful for several things. Color can attract attention, provided that it contrasts enough with the background (for example, a bright-yellow notice box on a white background). Color can express meaning. For example, red usually symbolizes danger or stopping (as at a traffic light) and so is best reserved for error messages; while green generally tends to mean success or an invitation to proceed and so should be used for content of this kind. Color can also highlight relationships, such as color coding things like buttons and toolbars to aid the user.

Keep in mind a couple of things when using color. First, different cultures will associate different things with colors, so make sure that any meaning you intend to communicate with your color selection works in your markets. Secondly, don't forget about color-blindness; take extra care when differentiating items through color, like bars on a chart. If a user is color-blind, they may not be able to distinguish between certain colors, most often red and green, so you may need to use other indicators, such as shape and texture, as well.

Contrast

How light or dark something is in relation to the elements around it will have an effect on the usability of an interface. The key here is contrast. Black text on a white background has a higher contrast, and is easier to spot and read, than gray text on a white background. Tuning down the contrast of certain elements allows you to fade them into the background, letting the user differentiate between more important and less important elements.

Texture

There is a concept in interactive design called *affordance*. Affordance is the quality that communicates to the user how something is meant to be used. Think of door handles. The best way to make a door that opens one way is to attach a handle on the pull side and leave a flat handle plate on the push side. People will know whether to push or pull automatically because the interface communicates how it should be used; i.e. it affords less methods of interaction and so focuses the user on the correct one.

We can translate this idea into user interface design on the screen with texture. For example, some elements in a visual interface may be draggable, like the corner of a window that lets you resize it. To indicate that you can click and drag it, a set of ridges usually appears on it, illustrating a rougher texture. Rough textures are often used to add a stronger grip surface to real-life objects to help us pull them with our fingers, and that idea is translated onto the screen, where instead of fingers you would use a mouse cursor.

Practical Techniques For Crafting Effective User Interfaces

We've talked about what user interfaces are, what characteristics all user interfaces should have and the core tools we can use to build them, so now let's look at some practical techniques you can use in your own Web applications and websites.

Use white space to build relationships

White space is the empty space between various content elements, such as headings, text and buttons. White space is a great tool for building relationship between different elements. By tightening the space between elements, you can form groupings of related items. Increasing the space between these groupings will further accentuate their connection by separating them from the rest of the content. Use white space to group related controls and to build a hierarchy of items on the page.

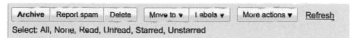

The Gmail toolbar features three groups of buttons separated by some white space. Each group features buttons that perform related actions.

Rounded corners define boundaries

Rounded corners are often used to improve the look and feel of graphical elements. They look nice and add that extra bit of visual polish to your interface; but that's not all they can be used for. Rounded corners define boundaries of objects. When you see a rounded corner, you know it is the

Notice how the rounded corners in Ballpark's clients list define the edges of each record. There are also corners in the middle of each record, but these are used as separators between related data rather than as edges of the overall container.

end of the container. If the corner is straight, it could be attached to another container, so the boundary is not as clear. Rounded corners, or any other visual corner treatment for that matter, can thus reinforce the boundaries of containers.

Convey meaning with color

Color is a great tool for communicating meaning; for example, to define different elements. You could, if you so choose, use color coding to distinguish between different types of buttons in your application. Red could be used for destructive buttons like delete and remove, blue could be used for standard buttons and green could be used for save and update actions. Color coding can also be used to distinguish between various pieces of user-created data on overview screens to make them easy to scan.

Direct attention

Use animation to draw attention. Sometimes, color and contrast alone aren't enough to attract a user's attention. If something crucial has happened, and you really must make sure the user has noticed it, use animation. The human eye is attuned to catching movement, especially on static backgrounds. If a user adds a to-do item to a list in a productivity application or adds a product to their shopping cart, use animation to highlight what has happened. For example, you could use a highlight effect when an item is created on the screen. This is especially useful for applications that

When you post a new message in Yammer, it combines slide-out and highlights animations.

Latest project activity

Task	Task closed – Make some coffee Change by dmitry_fadeyev, less than a minute ago
Task	Task created – Make some coffee Change by dmitry_fadeyev, less than a minute ago
Note	Note created – Hello world! Change by dmitry_fadeyev, 1 minute ago
Blog	Blog post created – New project created Change by dmitry_fadeyev, 1 minute ago
Project	Project created Change by dmitry_fadeyev, 1 minute ago

Goplan uses color-coded labels along the left side of its dashboard to allow users to quickly differentiate between different types of items, like tasks, notes and blog entries.

use AJAX heavily; in these cases, the page won't refresh when a particular action has been taken, so it's up to the interface to tell the user that something has happened.

Shadows and darkened backgrounds for focus

Another great way to focus user attention on an area is to use shadows and darkened backgrounds. Shadows can be used around pop-up menus and modal windows and act as blankets that block out visual noise around the window. Shadows decrease the contrast of elements that lie under them, which in turn increases the contrast of the items they're used for. Modal windows can also have a darker (or lighter) semi-transparent layer underneath, which also helps reduce the visual noise of the content it covers and so focuses the user's attention on the modal window itself.

Emphasize core actions

Many applications have screens that feature primary and secondary actions. For example, if you're creating a project in a project management application, the main form will probably have fields for the name of the project, the deadline, the priority level and so on. At the bottom, you may see a "Create" button. Often, you'll also see a "Cancel" button or link next to it. The cancel action is less important because your users usually won't need it, so you can decrease its visual "weight". For example, you could make "Create" a button and "Cancel" a simple hyperlink with no visual deco-

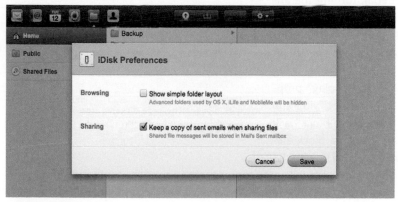

MobileMe darkens the background around modal windows and applies drop-shadows to them. This shifts the user's attention to the window by blocking out the noise below.

ration. This shifts the focus to the main action and helps the user locate it more quickly when they finish filling out the form.

More efficiency with block links

Use padded block links for easier cursor targeting. Web applications rely on HTML building blocks for their construction, which means they make heavy use of the anchor (better known as the "link") element. The anchor element is "inline" by default, which basically means that its width and height cover only the text inside it. This in turn means that the clickable area of the link is only as big as the text itself, which may be too small in many cases for users to comfortably click on. We can apply padding to the anchor element to make it larger.

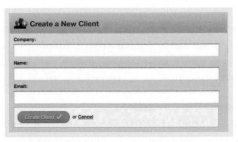

Notice how much more prominent the "Create Client" button is compared to "Cancel" on this Ballpark client creation form.

For links in a list, like in a sidebar, turning the anchors into "blocks" may be an even better solution. You can specify an element's type by using the CSS "display" property; so, specifying the anchor as a "block" will turn it into a block element, which means its height and width will no longer follow the size of the text inside it but will instead span the full width of its container by default. This is ideal for lists of links in a sidebar.

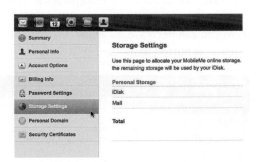

MobileMe uses padded links in its sidebar navigation panel. The large clickable areas allow you to position the mouse cursor over them faster, improving usability.

Use verbs as labels

When using your application, people will always be looking to do something. This means they'll be thinking in verbs. "I want to save this file", or "I want to update this entry". When building dialog boxes, or any other type of user prompt, use verbs rather than exclamations like "Yes", "No" and "Okay". When the user sees options like "Okay" and "Cancel", they will have to read the message above to understand what they're being asked to do. However, if you present the choices as verbs – for example, "Save", "Don't Save" and "Cancel" – you make the dialog and selections clear to the user without them even having to read the accompanying message.

Backpack makes great use of verbs for its buttons and links, ensuring clarity for each choice.

Auto-focus/re-focus on input

Form-oriented applications might benefit from automatically activating the main form's input field when the Web page loads. For example, search engines like Google focus on their main search field on the assumption that almost everyone arriving on their home page will want to type a search query into the input field, and so when the page loads you can start typing right away. Automatically activating input fields can work in other contexts: for example, in applications that require successive inputs, like a shopping-list builder. After the first item is entered, the user may want to enter more, so you should automatically re-focus on the input field to allow for quick, successive inputs.

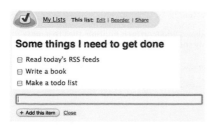

Tadalist allows for quick, successive input of to-do items. When you write a task and hit "Enter", the application adds the new item and then automatically focuses back on the text field, ready for more.

Use hover controls to simplify and de-clutter

Many applications have a set of context-sensitive controls, like buttons for deleting and editing individual records in a list. To make it easy to target something directly, they're usually placed next to each item, but this causes a lot of duplication. Most of the time the user won't need these controls, and when they do, they'll only need them for one particular item.

To simplify your interface, use hover controls, which only show up when you hover over a specific area. So, for example, when hovering over the record you want to edit, an edit button will show up, but the button will be hidden for all other records.

Hover controls are a great way to de-clutter and simplify interfaces, but you should consider a couple of things before implementing them. First, think about discoverability. People need to discover the user interface element before they can use it: are your controls prominent enough that a user would stumble on them? People naturally move the mouse around the screen and hover over items they're looking at, so this may not be a big issue but is still worth taking into account. Secondly, Web browsing interfaces on mobile devices like phones may not be able to simulate mouse cursor hovering, so these controls may be inaccessible.

Twitter shows the "Reply" and "Add to favorites" buttons when hovering over each message.

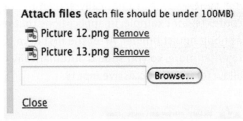

Basecamp allows you to attach multiple files to a message but only shows one attachment field at a time.

Expanding forms

If your form requires multiple data items to be entered into the same input fields – for example, attaching multiple files to a message or adding multiple people to a company record in your database – then you could use expanding forms to achieve this in an elegant fashion. Because the user only works with one field at a time, you should display only one field at a time to them. When they fill out and add a record, the application creates an extra input field below it to allow them to enter more information. This way, instead of displaying several empty input fields at once, you display only one empty field and add more as necessary.

Labels inside input fields

Simplifying interfaces depends mostly on thoughtful reduction. You want to cut out the unnecessary and make better use of space for the stuff that remains. One clever idea for forms is to put labels inside the actual input fields themselves. This saves space and also makes it dead clear to which field each label applies.

MobileMe compacts its log-in screen by moving text-field labels inside the text fields themselves.

Context-sensitive interface elements

Sometimes you need to integrate additional functionality for more experienced users of your application but don't want to add weight to the interface. What you can do is offer context-sensitive interface elements on demand. For example, if you have a search bar somewhere in your applic that has advanced filters, you could display just the search bar when it's not being used, and then reveal more controls when the user clicks on the box. This way, the interface remains slim, while the advanced functionality is only a click away.

Vimeo displays extended search filters when you hover over the search bar, giving more experienced users of the website a little extra functionality on demand.

Icons

Icons can be used to simplify the interface and make it look more visually appealing, but there are some considerations to take into account before you implement them. Icons are almost always less clear than words. Writing out a label is easy: you just say exactly what the button does. When designing an icon, however, you have to come up with an effective metaphor to describe the action in question. Also, the metaphor you choose may not translate very well in different countries if the illustration is of something local (even trash cans vary in appearance across the globe).

Icons work best when there aren't too many of them on the screen at the same time and each one is visually different enough from the others to stand out. This means that varying shape and color is key to building a successful set of icons. Implemented correctly, icons make the interface easier to use, because once users familiarize themselves with the icon set, the distinctive shapes and colors help them jump right to the icon they want.

Make it responsive with loading Indicators

Nobody likes waiting. Waiting means you're spending time doing nothing while you could be doing something valuable. Unfortunately, every application has features that take time to execute; whether it is exporting a large document or fetching the results of a search query, your users will

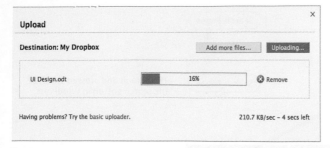

Upload		✕
Destination: My Dropbox	Add more files...	Uploading...
UI Design.odt	16%	✕ Remove
Having problems? Try the basic uploader.		210.7 KB/sec – 4 secs left

Dropbox shows a progress bar when users upload files using the Web interface. For events such as these, where wait times vary considerably, a progress bar is essential so that users don't have to keep guessing how much longer they will have to wait.

have to wait. But you can make the wait time feel considerably shorter by showing a loading indicator. Whenever something loads, add a loading indicator, such as a spinning animation or progress bar. Research shows that users perceive the wait time to be less when such indicators are displayed[2]. Loading indicators are great for short wait times, but what if an action takes a minute or more to complete? While you can't do anything about the load time itself (assuming you've already done everything in your power about that), you can do something about the waiting experience of your users. Take this time to entertain or inform. For example, many applications display interesting hints and tips during long wait times. If the user isn't doing anything productive, at least they can learn something new.

Make it responsive with pressed button states

The responsiveness of your application doesn't depend solely on the optimization of your back-end architecture. The way your user interface behaves plays a big part in this, too. One of the most used elements of any

OtherInbox has a set of icons for the main navigation bar, with labels under each one for clarity.

2 http://www.usabilitypost.com/2009/01/23/making-wait-times-feel-shorter/

User Interface Design in Modern We

The default and pressed states of the search button in WordPress.

Campaign Monitor provides a detailed help message when you first log in, as well as a large button that takes you to the campaign creation screen.

visual interface is the button. In desktop applications, buttons have several states, the most common being the default state, in which the button just sits there, and the pressed state when you click on it.

The pressed state looks just like that: the button appears to have been pressed. This state sends instant feedback to users that their click was successful. Just as on the desktop, pressed button states can be used in Web applications to provide that extra bit of feedback and responsiveness.

Helpful blank states

When a user loads your application for the first time, there likely won't be very much on the screen; the user hasn't entered any data yet, so there is nothing to display. Take this blank state as an opportunity to aid the user by including a short help message that provides information on how to get started. To make things even easier, you can provide a link right in the help message pointing to the action it recommends; so, for example, if your application is for managing email campaigns, and the user has just created a new account and logged in, the help message could provide a link to the creation page for new campaigns.

Advertise features

Your users won't know your application inside out, so in some situations it may be a good idea to advertise features in the application itself. Also, because Web applications tend to be updated constantly and substantial new features are introduced from time to time, it makes sense to inform your users about them. Do this by placing a small notice in a prominent area of the screen. It should be fairly eye-catching but not distract or handicap the user in performing their tasks. The users should also be able to close the notice once they've read it.

> **The conversation has been moved to the Trash.** Learn more Undo

Gmail displays this undo message each time you delete an email, allowing you to get it back quickly.

Undo

One of the most relied-on features in desktop applications is the trusty undo shortcut. Accidently changed the formatting of that chart you're working on? No problem: hit Ctrl/Cmd and Z on your keyboard, and the application takes a step back and restores the document to its state before your last action. Undo is a crucial tool in forgiving interfaces, and it can be used in Web applications as well. For example, you could either integrate the familiar keyboard shortcut or show temporary notice messages with undo links in them.

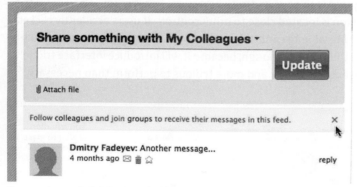

Yammer shows a helpful note under the main input area regarding the "follow" feature. Once the users read it, they can close it using the little cross icon on the right.

You have deleted this writeboard:

"Very important notes"

An email has been sent to <u>example@email.com</u> with a link to recover this writeboard. The recovery link will work for 2 months, after which the writeboard will be permanently deleted.

Writeboard allows you to restore your work for up to two months after deleting it.

Restore

People often change their mind after deleting something, so it's wise to implement some extra protective measures when dealing with the more important bits of data in your application; for example, project files in a project management application. When a user deletes a project, you could, instead of deleting it right away, archive it for a certain amount of time. If they change their mind and decide they need the project files back, you will be able to restore them easily. A few extra megabytes of used space is worth the trade-off for making your customers really happy when they discover that all is not lost.

Confirmation dialogs

When allowing destructive actions in your application, such as deletion of items, it is a good idea to provide a confirmation dialog to ensure that the user really wants to go ahead with his action. This is more important if the delete button is located close to other controls; if users accidently click it, they should be able to cancel the action before it happens. Be careful not to overuse this feature, though, because it will introduce interface friction by making actions longer and more tedious to perform than necessary.

Freckle uses a confirmation dialog to make sure you don't delete entries by accident.

Conclusion

There is a Japanese philosophy called Kaizen, which focuses on continuous improvement through small, gradual steps. User interface design, especially in modern Web applications, doesn't have to be in a finished state because you can always keep evolving and improving it. Think of it like Kaizen.

The old model of distributing software on CDs carried a big downside: once you burned and shipped the product, you couldn't change it ... well, not very easily. You could release a patch, but your users would have to download and install it before any changes took effect, and you couldn't guarantee that everyone would update. Additionally, releasing a patch for every small change wasn't feasible, so you pretty much had to get things as perfect as possible the first time, which required a lot of testing before the release. The software-as-a-service model changed all that. The benefit of hosting your Web application online is that you can deploy little changes whenever you want, and all of your users will instantly gain access to them.

This means you don't have to get your interface 100% right the first time. If something doesn't work, you can change it. By observing how users interact with your interface, you will begin to get a good feel for how well it works and where the friction is – where things slow your users down. If any parts of the UI need improvement, you can update them for all of your users very easily. This is the Kaizen approach to interface design: small, gradual, regular improvements. So don't worry about getting things perfect the first time; instead, iterate as you go, and you'll soon end up with a great interface that has evolved through real usage. ∎

The

Art

And

Science

of CSS-Layouts

Jacob Gube and Kayla Knight

I n modern Web design, the craft of developing a website's layout requires patience, precision and solid knowledge of CSS. While design elements determine flow and hierarchy within the design, Web layouts build up the skeleton of the website, providing space and a structure in which the design elements can breathe and serve their role. But laying out a page is often tricky and time-consuming and can be undermined by browser inconsistencies and all sorts of trade-offs between various types and styles of layouts.

Good news: there are some practical guidelines that can help you approach these issues manageably and effectively. This article throws light on various kinds of layouts, shows their advantages and disadvantages and suggests situations in which each would work best. We'll also talk about the main techniques and related issues for gaining a better understanding of CSS layouts in general.

Good news: there are some practical guidelines that can help you approach these issues manageably and effectively.

The search for a "holy", universal layout usually boils down to comparing existing approaches and will be heavily influenced by the designer's skills and choice between pixel-perfect designs and adaptive, flexible ones. Essentially, designers have a choice of four major layout types: **fixed-width, fluid, elastic** and **hybrid**. These names refer to each layout's ability (or inability) to adjust its dimensions (primarily its width) according to the user's browser size.

Fixed-Width Layout

A fixed-width layout, as the name suggests, is a static layout whose width is set to a certain fixed value, in pixel units. Such layouts have a wrapper of a fixed width, and all components inside it have percentage or fixed widths. The designer has more control over the placement of design elements around the content areas and can work with content and navigation widths more precisely. Typography, graphics and proportions between website elements can be exactly pre-defined by the designer using general heuristics and rules of thumb. Fixed width ensures that these proportions always hold true and that the overall design remains the same, no matter what screen resolution the visitor has.

Fixed-width layouts are a popular choice because they are simple, intuitive and easy to implement and customize. With a fixed-width layout, you are assured that the design will look the same at different screen resolutions, so you don't have to play a guessing game, and development time is reduced because of the fewer requirements for designing and for testing under various conditions. Specifically, these layouts work with straightforward "absolute" values (pixels), which many designers find more comfortable and intuitive to work with than percentage or em units. Pixel-perfect positioning of blocks of content is probably the most obvious advantage of working with this layout type.

The width of this layout is usually determined by average screen resolutions. Currently, most users have resolutions that display at 1024 × 768 pixels or more, so most designers will use between 960 and 1050 pixels for their layout's width, which lets the user avoid having to scroll horizontally and gives ample leeway for the 20-pixel vertical scroll bar found in most Web browsers. Still, it's important to notice that smaller screen resolutions may require a horizontal scroll bar, depending on the fixed layout's width.

Colourpixel's portfolio has a layout whose width is fixed at 950 pixels. This is how it looks with the browser's view port set at 1045 pixels.

An advantage of fixed-width layouts is that design elements are easier to position and things are more predictable. Positioning elements is not complicated when you're certain of the width of your layout. Besides, even if a website is designed to be compatible with the smallest screen resolution, 800 × 600, the content will still be wide enough at a larger resolution to be easily legible. Print designers who make the jump to Web-based media tend to choose fixed-width layouts because of the precise control of presentation they are afforded – after all, absolute positioning of elements is very common in print design.

Here is the same website at a different resolution: the browser's viewport, at 1680 pixels, displays empty space to the right of the layout.

A disadvantage of fixed-width layouts is that they don't take advantage of the user's full browser area. Of course, screen resolution is not necessarily the same as the browser window's resolution, because many "widescreen" users do not maximize their browser window[1]. However, if a user has a large wide-screen display (for example, a resolution of 1900 × 1200, and a browser resolution of 1500 pixels), it is reasonable to assume that a relatively large portion of the screen area is not being used. For instance, a fixed-width layout of 750 pixels on this display would leave empty space that is as wide horizontally as the layout itself!

1   As screen resolutions increase with high-resolution monitors, users generally tend to avoid browsing in full-screen mode. In many cases, an application is running beside the browsing area (such as a Twitter app, RSS feed reader or IM client), while the browser window itself sports a variety of extensions. See also "50.4% of respondents maximise windows" (456bereastreet.com).

Consequently, a fixed-width layout may create excessive white space, thus upsetting "divine proportion", the "Rule of Thirds", overall balance and similar design principles. Furthermore, seamless textures, patterns and image continuation are needed to accommodate those with larger resolutions. At the very least, centering the wrapper DIV is highly recommended, to maintain a sense of balance in the fixed-width design:

```
#wrapper { margin: 0 auto; }
```

will do the trick. Or else, for users with large screen resolutions, the entire layout would be tucked away in the left upper corner.

And then there's the big question of what the appropriate width is. Many users have large wide-screen monitors, but most have average-sized monitors, and some have still yet smaller screen resolutions. In any case, most users adjust the window to their preferred size and do not necessarily have maximized, standardized or proportional screen resolutions.

In practice, finding the "right" balance for a website's fixed-width layout usually requires a thorough study of the profile of that particular website's average user. Assessing your visitors' browsing preferences and then leveraging your design accordingly is always a good idea. The most common way to do that is to analyze your website's statistics to see which resolutions are the most prevalent and how many users use small screens. As a rule of thumb, you can usually create a good user experience by keeping the width of your layout to between 800 and 1000 pixels. As professionals, we have to create layouts for our visitors, not ourselves, even if that means that our designs look terrible on our own high-resolution wide-screen laptops.

Let's create a simple two-column fixed-width layout, with a header section for the logo and primary navigation and a footer for additional website information. The HTML would be as follows:

```
<div id="container">

  <div id="header">

    <!-- logo, navigation -->

  </div>
```

```
<div id="content">

  <!-- main content -->

</div>

<div id="sidebar">

  <!-- sidebar -->

</div>

<div id="footer">

  <!-- site information -->

</div>

</div>
```

To make the width fixed, we set a width on the #container DIV. We also assign a fixed width to the left and right columns. To make the header and footer equal to the container's width, we give them a width property of 100% (which is unnecessary most of the

You can see a fixed-width layout on the website 24 ways. The #content DIV is fixed at 900 pixels.

time but good practice nonetheless if we want to make sure they are indeed equal to the width of the container).

We use the "float" property to display the left and right columns beside each other (of course, we could use relative or absolute positioning instead) and the "clear" property for the footer so that it displays below the two columns. Note that you would need to use some kind of global browser reset to ensure a cross-browser presentation of the layout.

```
#container {

  margin: 0 auto; /* Centering the layout horizontally */

  width: 960px;

}

#header {

  width: 100%;

}

#content {

  width: 600px;

  float: left;

  display: inline; /* IE 5/6 Doubled Float Margin Bug */

}

#sidebar {

  width: 330px;
/* 960px - 600px - 330px = 30px is used to separate columns */

  float. right;

  display: inline; /* IE 5/6 Doubled Float-Margin Bug */

}

#footer {

  width: 100%;

  clear: both;

}
```

Choosing between a fixed-width layout and another type is a question of how much freedom the designer is willing to give the user. The former entails that design decisions are more in the hands of the designer than

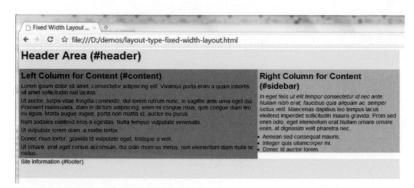

An example of a fixed-width layout.

the user, while the latter entails that components like fonts, images and columns will scale fluidly according to the user's preferences.

A common argument against fixed-width layouts is the difficulty of maintaining the code over a long period of time. If your design has a fixed size for the fonts in design elements (even if IE6 users cannot rescale the text at all), and your client requests a bigger size for certain design elements (for example, the text), you could end up with a "nightmare of changes and recalculations for an extra pixel on the text size" (The Fallacy of Page Zooming, *allinthehead.com*). A better approach would be to use relationships between elements to determine the essence of design proportions (i.e. using relative values). This is exactly where flexible (fluid and elastic) layouts come into play.

Fluid (Liquid) Layout

A layout with a fluid width, also known as a liquid layout, adjusts its width in proportion to the size of the Web browser's view port. In such layouts, the majority of the elements inside the container are defined in percentage values, using the current properties of the browser window as the baseline. When the size of the browser window changes, so does the layout, because the baseline is changing with the user's every adjustment of the browser window. In other words, the widths of individual layout blocks adjust automatically according to the user's browser window. So, if a user is not quite comfortable with the line length of an article she is reading, she can simply resize the browser window, and the content block will shrink automatically.

In such layouts, the relationships between layout elements play an important role, because the widths of child elements set in percentage values are always determined by their parent elements (not adjacent elements!). For instance, if the width of the layout container (whose parent is the browser window) is set at 90%, and the width of the navigation block within the container is set at 80%, then the width of the navigation element is 72% of the browser area ($1 \times 0.9 \times 0.8 = 0.72$). As you can see, coding for such layouts requires a profound understanding of the structure of the design; designers may be more prone to error when working with this layout type, but a successful execution will make the website more flexible and adaptable for some end users[2].

Unlike fixed-width layouts, liquid layouts give users the freedom to decide the width of the layout they are viewing.

Fluid layouts can take up a lot of the available screen space in browsers, making it possible for designers to distribute content evenly and with adequate white space. If designed properly, a layout will have a consistent amount of white space, regardless of the browser or screen resolution in which it is viewed, making the design more consistent and user-friendly. Also, such layouts can eliminate the obtrusive horizontal scroll bar when viewed in smaller resolutions.

Unlike fixed-width layouts, liquid layouts give users the freedom to decide the width of the layout they are viewing. With them, designers move away from rigid, consistently pixel-perfect layouts to a more flexible (and therefore riskier) environment in which the proportions between certain website elements are more abstract and difficult to define. No wonder that many designers avoid them. They take the predictability of positioning design elements with pixel-level accuracy out of the designer's hands.

2 Of course, many end users do not know that they can resize the browser to adjust the line length, but that is a topic for another discussion.

Because designers work with relative percentage values instead of absolute pixel values, they will often have to round some values up or down in practice (for example, from 15.433333% to 15.43% or 15%), making the design less precise[3]. While smoothing the values over works fine for smaller resolutions, the practice can result in quirky side-effects at larger resolutions, such as creating noticeable gaps in the layout or making the content area too wide and thus hard to read.

In fact, the latter result is the most significant downside of fluid-width layouts. Because the width of content is determined by the user's view port, users with wide-screen resolutions will likely find that bodies of text have line lengths so long that reading them becomes cumbersome and uncomfortable. And if a particular page with a fluid width doesn't have much text on

In fact, the latter result is the most significant downside of fluid-width layouts.

it, the user may end up seeing only a couple of lines of text in the content area and a disproportionately tall vertical sidebar column with a huge amount of white space around it.

To solve this problem, designers often set a maximum width for the content block, thereby forcing a more or less optimal width for the layout. To determine the maximum width of a #content-block, many designers aim for optimal readability (47 to 86 characters per line) plus 10%. A minimum width is rarely set and only if the readability of the design would significantly suffer at smaller screen resolutions.

In CSS, the maximum width of a layout is defined using the "max-width" CSS property. The property is supported by all popular browsers (IE 7+, Firefox 1+, Safari 2+, Opera 9.2+), except, of course, Internet Explorer 6.

However, there is a workaround for IE6 and below. Notice that, as of version 8, Internet Explorer no longer supports Microsoft's proprietary dynamic

3 Of course, it depends on the designer's ability to select reasonable width values for containers or to use more exotic numerical values to calculate the width of the layout's elements. For the record, according to W3C's specifications, using real number values in CSS (such as 82.345%) is okay, but you cannot be sure that it will be rounded and rendered identically in all modern browsers, which is why integer values are often preferred.

properties (MSDN IE Blog "Ending Expressions"), also known as CSS expressions, so the IE6 bugfix will not affect newer IE versions. Dynamic properties, which allow you to use JavaScript logic such as control structures and mathematical computations, are discussed by Web developer Svend Tofte in the context of solving the "max-width" issue in Internet Explorer browsers. One can limit the width of the #content-block in the following example (*svendtofte.com*):

```
#content {

max-width: 30em;

width: expression(

    document.body.clientWidth > (500/12) *

        parseInt(document.body.currentStyle.fontSize)?

        "30em":

        "auto" );
}
```

The user's font-size settings – in points (pt) – are checked against the body's width. Tofte determined, arbitrarily based on experimentation, that at 500 pixels the default 12-point font gets wider than 30 ems, which is what his layout width is set to.

Working backwards, if the body's width is greater than the ratio of 500 pixels to 12 points multiplied by the user's font setting, then you set the width of the element to a maximum of 30 ems; otherwise, you let it adjust its width automatically (hence the "auto").

The downside of this technique is that, because dynamic properties are not included in W3C's CSS 2 specifications, it invalidates your CSS. But depending on your situation, that may be a small price to pay for offering users of what is still one of the most popular browsers on the market support for liquid layouts with minimum and maximum widths.

The Clearleft website is an example of a fluid-width layout. The two images above show the website at a width of 1280 pixels and at 800 pixels. Notice

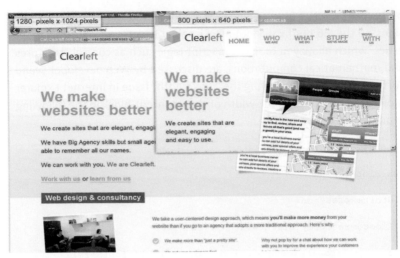

The Clearleft website is an example of a fluid-width layout. The two images above show the website at a width of 1280 pixels and at 800 pixels. Notice how the content area adjusts the "We make websites better" slogan, wrapping it to three lines at 800 pixels and only two lines at 1280 pixels.

how the content area adjusts the "We make websites better" slogan, wrapping it to three lines at 800 pixels and only two lines at 1280 pixels. Instead of two, it takes just one line.

Finally, let's code a simple, pure two-column fluid layout, using the same HTML structure as the one in the fixed-layout example. Note again that you would need to use some kind of global browser reset to ensure a cross-browser presentation of the layout.

```
#container {

  margin: 0 auto;

  width: 75%;

}

#header {

  width: 100%;
```

```
}

#content {

  width: 60%;

  float: left;

  display: inline; /* IE 5/6 Doubled Float-Margin Bug */

}

#sidebar {

  width: 40%;

  float: right;

  display: inline; /* IE 5/6 Doubled Float-Margin Bug */

}

#footer {

  width:100%;

  clear:both;

}
```

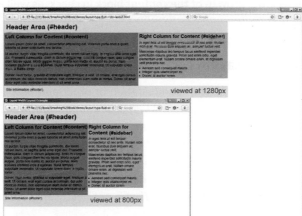

Here is a fluid layout tested in two Web browsers, one with a width of 1280 pixels, and the other with a width of 800 pixels, with the container width set to 75% of the browser's view port.

To determine the optimal width for a liquid layout, it is reasonable to use "width: auto" or any percentage value to make sure that the layout takes up the available width of the browser window automatically. For a minimum width, you could use a pixel value (like 760px); this lower limit could be used for all fluid layouts, so that the content remains readable even at the smallest screen resolution. For the maximum width, common practice is to use an em value (like 90em), so that the text width doesn't get out of control but remains constant at various screen resolutions. A pleasant side effect: the maximum width is scaled according to the font size of the browser.

A classic way to calculate proportion is to divide the font size of a given element in pixels by the font size of its container (that is, its context).

When implementing fluid layouts, use percentage values for the margins and padding of text elements (relative to the view port's width, of course), so that when the window is resized, the margins and padding adjust, keeping the proportions consistent and their size flexible. This technique has been called "concertina padding" a term coined by Richard Rutter ("Web Standards Group: Ten Questions for Richard Rutter", *webstandardsgroup. org*). When the page is resized, the margins and padding resize as well, keeping the growth of the content block in check, as well as the length of the text lines.

Fluid Grid Layouts

Grid-based design is a manifestation of order and precision. Essentially, grids allow for a strategic and systematic organization of typography and design elements, using alignment, symmetry and proper spacing; they contribute to creating designs that are pleasing to read and easy to scan. Grid layouts can be implemented in various layout types, but designers often assume that flexible layouts in particular are difficult or impossible to pair with traditional grid systems. That is not necessarily the case.

Essentially, a fluid grid layout can be created through a smart use of DIV layers, percentages and very simple math. The idea comes from Ethan

Marcotte (Fluid Grids, *alistapart.com*), who realized that "if we could treat font sizes not as pixels, but as proportions measured against their container, we could do the same with the different elements draped across our grid". His basic idea is to use relative units, namely percentages, and a simple division formula to find the equivalents of pixel widths that would normally be used for fixed-width design. Because em units in typography

Grid-based design is a manifestation of order and precision. Essentially, grids allow for a strategic and systematic organization of typography and design elements.

are all about context, other elements in the overall layout could be considered the same. As Ethan points out, "this will allow us to convert our design's pixel-based widths into percentages, and keep the proportions of our grid intact as it resizes".

A classic way to calculate proportion is to divide the font size of a given element in pixels by the font size of its container (that is, its context). As a result, we get the desired proportion, expressed in relative, em- or percentage-friendly terms. We get a quite obvious yet very helpful formula: target ÷ context = result.

Now, if we apply this formula to a design, we should end up with a solid fluid layout. However, we actually want a grid layout, so we start out by creating a well-defined fixed-width grid with seven columns of 124 pixels each, separated by 20 pixel-wide gutters, all of which adds up to a width of 988 pixels.

Let's assume now that we have a 700 pixel-width <h1> element in our layout (which spans five columns and four gutters between them: 5 × 124 pixels + 4 × 20 pixels = 700 pixels). This element should be a block element and should be centered in the layout (which means having the overall horizontal margin of 288 pixels, 144 pixels on the left side and 144 pixels on the right side).

To calculate the width of <h1> in relative units, we simply divide 700 pixels (the target) by 988 pixels (the context), giving us 700 ÷ 988 = 0.7085. 0.7085 translates to 70.85%, which we can put directly in our style sheet:

```
h1 {

    width: 70.85%;              /* 700px / 988px = 0.7085 */

}
```

Of course, we also need to take care of the margins. Because the left margin is supposed to be 144 pixels (the target), we can again apply our formula to derive its relative width in the container (the context): 144 ÷ 988 = 0.14575, which translates to 14.575%. Finally, we get:

```
h1 {

    margin-left: 14.575%;    /* 144px / 988px = 0.14575 */

    width: 70.85%;           /* 700px / 988px = 0.7085 */

}
```

What remains is to apply this formula the same way to all layout elements, and we will end up with a solid, flexible, fluid grid. This is a very

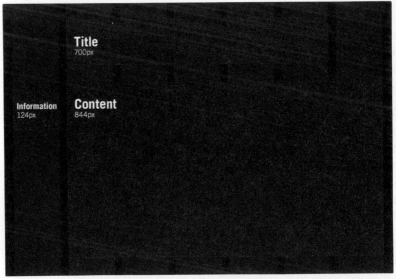

A simple grid layout with a title, information and large content block.

easy concept and a much more efficient way to handle proportions in fluid design. With this technique, a designer doesn't have the excuse that proportions cannot be maintained or that they ruin the aesthetic appeal of their layouts.

Designers determine the length of margins in different ways. One way is to calculate the percentages of the margins (in this case, 20 pixels ÷ 880 pixels). Another is to set fixed margins or, as in our example, hard-code them as 20 pixels.

Each method has its pros and cons. With percentage margins, the designer risks making the margins too wide in very large screen resolutions but probably achieves better proportion. Fixed margins may cause slight imperfections in the proportions but guarantee that the spacing will look right no matter what the screen size is.

Adaptive Fluid (Liquid) Layouts

A common problem with fluid designs is that, even though they adapt to many screen resolutions, if the resolution is too small (such as on a phone or PDA) or incredibly large, things start to look a bit funny. For example, a three-column layout would look very cluttered on a PDA screen whose resolution is only 240 pixels wide. On the other hand, if the "min-width" property is used, the layout may contain a horizontal scroll bar and look unreadable.

To address this problem, we can use a technique that involves adapting content to specific ranges of screen resolutions. This is where the name "adaptive fluid layout" comes from. We can create slightly different custom layouts for resolutions that are 640 to 800 pixels, 320 to 640 pixels, 240 to 320 pixels and 240 pixels and below, respectively. Likewise, custom adjustments could be made for screen resolutions that are 800 to 1024 pixels, 1024 to 1280 pixels and 1280 pixels and up, respectively.

The benefits are obvious: the designer is able to leverage a layout's look at different resolutions with greater accuracy. The tiniest and largest resolutions can be handled perfectly, while better adhering to design principles of spacing and balance, no matter what platform the design is being viewed on.

To create this type of layout, we need two things: separate style sheets for every range of screen resolutions, and a way of determining a user's screen resolution. The first step is to create a set of alternative layout files. For example, one file could be called narrow.css and would be tailored to very narrow resolutions. Another could be normal.css and would apply to conventional computer screen resolutions, and a third could be wide.css and would handle unusually large resolutions.

The benefits of adaptive layouts are obvious: the designer is able to leverage a layout's look at different resolutions with greater accuracy.

We can then use JavaScript to make some simple alterations depending on the preset style sheets: for example, using Kevin Hale's "Dynamic Resolution-Dependent Layout Technique" (*particletree.com*) or Marc Van Den Dobblesteen's "Switchy McLayout" (*alistapart.com*). Declarations of all the style sheets and the JavaScript file are then put in the header, just like in any other type of layout.

```
<!-- Narrow style sheet -->

<link rel="alternate stylesheet" type="text/css" href="css/
narrow.css" title="narrow" />

<!-- Default style sheet -->

<link rel="stylesheet" type="text/css" href="css/normal.css"
title="default" />

<!-- Wide style sheet -->

<link rel="alternate stylesheet" type="text/css" href="css/
wide.css" title="wide" />

<!-- Included JavaScript to switch style sheets -->
```

```
<script src="scripts/dynamiclayout.js" type="text/
javascript"></script>
```

Notice the title attribute in all three links to the style sheets: "narrow", "default" and "wide". Taking a closer look at the DynamicLayout() function in the JavaScript source, we can see that it is quite easy to customize which style sheet is called according to each title attribute. We can also see how to change the pixel widths accordingly.

```
function dynamicLayout(){

    var browserWidth = getBrowserWidth();

    // Narrow CSS rules

    if (browserWidth < 640)

    changeLayout("narrow");

    }

    // Normal (default) CSS rules

    if ((browserWidth >= 640) && (browserWidth <= 960))}

    changeLayout("default");

    }

    // Wide CSS rules

    if (browserWidth > 960){

    changeLayout("wide");

    }

}
```

Notice that because adaptive fluid layouts rely on JavaScript, they require users to have JavaScript enabled so that it can detect the monitor's resolution and serve the appropriate style sheet.

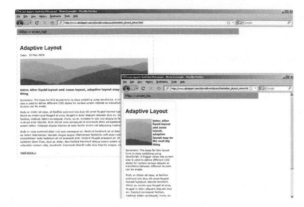

In the above image, you can see a demonstration of Switchy McLayout viewed at different Web browser sizes. The layout automatically adjusts as you resize the browser.

"Variable fixed-width layout" is a similar technique developed by Richard Rutter, based on Simon Collison's width-based layout (which he discusses in the article "Redesign Notes 1: Width-Based Layout", *colly.com*). As the

Richard Rutter's variable fixed-width layout uses JavaScript to automatically scale the layout, including the typography, on the fly. Viewed at 1280 pixels, the layout is a four-column layout, but shrunk down to 850 pixels (as seen in the view port), the layout automatically becomes a three-column layout, with the fourth-column shifting down.

screen resizes, so does the layout and typography. The change in layout size happens in real time, so if you were to resize your Web browser, the layout would adapt to your new size.

As pointed out above, a common problem with fluid layouts is that the text gets either so stretched or squished that the layout loses readability. Very narrow screens seem to create the biggest problem by causing big gaps in the text, but either extreme can frustrate users equally. Max-width and min-width are possible solutions, but when these properties are applied, the layout simply reverts to a partially fixed-width layout, and we lose the overall flexibility. Tinned Fruit's text-zooming technique (*tinnedfruit.com*) is based on a JavaScript that automatically resizes text based on the width of the user's screen. As the screen gets wider, the text gets larger. Likewise, as the screen gets thinner, the text gets smaller. In addition to this basic functionality, a designer can set a maximum and minimum text size so that the user never sees any odd-sized text. Furthermore, the designer can choose which elements should and should not be affected by the text zoom.

You can add the text-zooming JavaScript to a Web page externally. Below the external script line, simply insert the following code, modified as necessary:

```
<script type="text/javascript">

    var contentZoom = new TextZoom(

    "Content", // Reference element

    "Content", // Target element

    0.22, // Zoom ratio

    70, // Minimum font size (%)

    130); // Maximum font size (%)

    addLoadEvent(textZoomInit);

</script>
```

Text Zooming

Example Navigation Doesn't Resize

Sizing text with the browser window

**Resize this window. If you have javascript turned on, the text si
and navigation will not.**

Here's a simple DOM scripting technique for sizing text content
element, or any other element for that matter, including the doc

- maintain a (relatively) consistent reading line length in conte
- design a zoom layout that sizes text according to the viewpo
- maintain more control over content layout for varying viewpo

Features include:

- honours relative browser text size preferences
- minimum and maximum sizes to stop things getting silly
- no additional markup or CSS

Text-zoom technique: here is a
portion of the maximized page
(large width) that displays larger
text.

Text Zooming

Example Navigation Doesn't Resize

Sizing text with the browser window

**Resize this window. If you have javascript turned on, the text size in this
column *should* resize. The header and navigation will not.**

Here's a simple DOM scripting technique for sizing text content depending on
the width of its containing element, or any other element for that matter,
including the document body. This is useful if you want to:

- maintain a (relatively) consistent reading line length in content columns
- design a zoom layout that sizes text according to the viewport window
- maintain more control over content layout for varying viewport sizes

Features include:

- honours relative browser text size preferences
- minimum and maximum sizes to stop things getting silly
- no additional markup or CSS

Text-zoom technique: the same
page as above, except minimized to about 700 pixels in
width. The text is resized along
with the browser. Notice that
the text in the navigation at the
top is not resized.

A similar technique was suggested by Soh Tanaka in his article "Smart
Columns with CSS and jQuery" (*sohtanaka.com*). The technique is based
on a script that alters the width of DIVs for the best viewing experience,
and it also determines how many columns can be viewed across the page
in the browser's current size. The script removes any left-over white space

from the ends of columns (which may have been caused by the browser's width) and then redistributes it evenly throughout the columns using jQuery. The technique is perfect for users who resize their browsers, and does not simply treat browsers indiscriminately: a good example of an adaptive fluid layout.

Elastic (Zoomable) Layouts

When viewing a website with a fluid layout, the content can get so wide that the text becomes difficult to read. To improve readability, designers tend to limit the maximum width of a layout using CSS properties. An elastic (or zoomable) layout is a different approach that achieves the same goal; the basic idea is that designers adjust the width of the layout based on the user's font size rather than the browser's view port.

A pixel is an unscalable dot on a computer screen, whereas an em is a square unit of font size. Font sizes vary, and the em is a relative unit that adjusts to users' text-size preferences (Elastic Design, *alistapart.com*). Consequently, designers size fonts in em units relative to the font-size value of their parent elements. By using ems for both layout blocks and text elements, designers are able to make a Web layout scale consistently, maintain optimal line length for the body copy and create realistic zoom effects. The result: when the user increases the font size, the layout stretches automatically, just as you would expect from an elastic object.

Because the layout width doesn't depend on the browser's view port, elastic layouts behave similarly to fixed-width layouts, and they also inherit their advantages and disadvantages. A major increase in the browser's font size can make the layout explode in width and height, making the page completely unusable and unreadable. However, this will rarely happen, because a three-time increase in font size is not very common (especially if the designer uses a large enough font size as the base line for text elements).

As with fluid layouts, one of the most difficult things to grasp when starting out with elastic layouts is the math involved in calculating the proper em values. To simplify the conversion from pixels to ems, you can set the base value of the body's font size to 0.625 em, or 62.5% (because the default font size of most browsers is 16 pixels[4], and 10 pixels is exactly 62.5% of 16 pixels), which comes out to 10 pixels, making the calculation of the font size of child elements easier. For example, by setting the font size in the main body area to 0.625 em, you can set a DIV container that should be 960 pixels in width to 96 em; and so a <p> element there whose font size would otherwise be 12 pixels would now be 1.2 em.

One issue with elastic layouts, or layouts whose widths are adjusted based on font sizes, is the presentation of multimedia content, such as images and Flash objects. This adds complexity to elastic layouts, because in order for all elements in the layout to maintain their proportion, they must scale as the font size increases. Elastic layouts sometimes allow for all of their elements to scale; in other words, images will scale up or down in proportion to the layout, depending on the user's settings.

> One issue with elastic layouts is the presentation of multimedia content, such as images and Flash objects.

Of course, this can be done by giving images percentage-based width and height property values, such as <img width="80%" height="80%" alt="Image" />. Remember, though, that scaling up images with very small resolutions using percentage values will decrease their quality, because the browser would perform a "simulated" zoom, resulting in pixellated and blurry images. Besides, the browser would load the entire (large) images from the server and rescale them, thus increasing the server load and delaying the page loading time. Therefore, most designers always use absolute pixel values for images.

Another solution, described in Harvey Kane's article "Automatic Magazine Layout" (*alistapart.com*) requires some math and PHP. The title derives from how images are displayed in magazines: organized and always perfectly aligned. Consider the following PHP script:

```
# include the class file
```

---

4   16 pixels is a widely adopted default browser font size, but some people may change it or have the dpi on their machines set to 120 instead of 96, which would make all of the text on their system bigger.

```php
require_once('magazinelayout.class.php');

# Define the width for the output area (pixels)

$width = 600;

# Define padding around each image; this *must* be included
# in your style sheet (pixels)

$padding = 3;

# Define your template for outputting images
# (Don't forget to escape the &)

$template = '<img src="image.php?size=[size]&file=[image]"

alt="Screenshot" />';

# create a new instance of the class

$mag = new magazinelayout($width,$padding,$template);

# Add the images in any order

$mag->addImage( 'landscape1.jpg' );

$mag->addImage( 'portrait1.jpg' );

$mag->addImage( 'landscape2.jpg' );

# display the output

echo $mag->getHtml();
```

We can pre-define the width that we'd like our entire magazine-inspired image layout to render as. So, if we can determine the user's browser width, we can figure out how wide our image layout should be. This is easy enough, because we've already done it with our second technique: Fluid layouts with adaptive content. In his script, Kevin Hale uses a method called getBrowserWidth(). You can get an in-depth look at the code for this method in his article.

If we can use this method to retrieve the browser's width as a number, then we can use that number to find the pixel width of our content area (or whatever other area these images are going to be placed in). Let's say we'd like to put the images in our content area, which is set to a 70% width. Using simple math, we just need to figure out how many pixels is 70% of the browser's width.

Pixel width = Percentage of Content Area × Browser Width
$width = 0.70 × getBrowserWidth();

This is, of course, pretty basic math, and it is a pretty basic solution for dealing with images in fluid layouts, once the initial PHP script is set up. Adjust the PHP script to automatically find the pixel width of the images, and you've got a great way of dealing with images, or any other content that has a set width, in a fluid layout.

The main advantage of the elastic layout is its ability to always keep the proportions of design elements, ensuring proper readability and positioning. Elastic layouts are often the first choice for designers who want a compromise between fluid and fixed designs; the pros of each are found in elastic layouts. However, this layout type is more difficult to implement, and a lot of savvy and testing is often needed to get the layout right for most users.

Let's try a simple two-column elastic layout using the same HTML structure we used before. If we know that 1 em equals 16 pixels, then a width of 960 pixels equals 60 em. The left column at 600 pixels translates to 37.5 em, and the right column at 360 pixels translates to 22.5 em. To make it easier, here's the formula for calculating widths: 1 em ÷ 16 px × (width in pixels) = em equivalent.

```
#container {

    width: 60em;

}
```

```
#header {

    width: 60em;

}

#leftCol {

    width: 37.5em;

    float: left;

    display: inline; /* IE 5/6 Doubled Float-Margin Bug */

}

#rightCol {

    width: 22.5em;

    float: right;

    display: inline; /* IE 5/6 Doubled Float-Margin Bug */

}

#footer {

    width: 60em;

    clear: both;

}
```

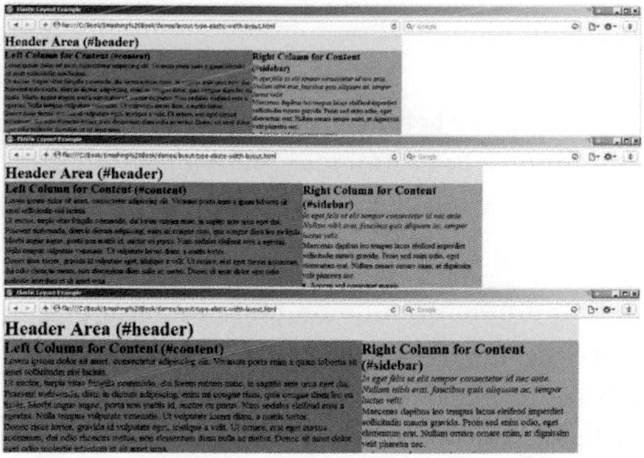

An elastic layout viewed at different text sizes, showing how the width of the layout increases as the text size increases.

The design community is divided in a heated disagreement about the viability of flexible layouts. The new generation of Web browsers – Firefox 3+, Opera 9.5+ and Internet Explorer 7+ – comes with a feature that seems will save Web developers a lot of work in future, namely the **full-page zoom.**

Instead of simply increasing and decreasing the font size of a website, browsers now enable users to literally scale the rendered layout, including visuals and background images. The whole design layout is scaled proportionally according to a set zoom factor, with all elements of a page's layout expanding equally. Consequently, every fixed pixel-based layout becomes "scalable"; content always remains within the layout area it is supposed to be in, and there is no chance of boxes overlapping each other, as we saw in previous generations of Web browsers. Intuitively, this leads to the conclusion that elastic layouts will become obsolete and will have outlived their purpose, because they achieve the same effect with counter-intuitive CSS code.

However, this is not true. As Zoe Mickley Gillenwater points out ("Why Browser Zoom Shouldn't Kill Flexible Layouts", *zomigi.com*), if you offer users a fixed-width layout with page zoom, they will sometimes see different number of characters per line than what you intended (for example, some people may increase the size because of vision problems).

It is also harder to preserve design proportions, because variable text sizes make it hard to predict where content will be displayed on a fixed-width page. Besides, while page zoom increases (and decreases) the overall layout of the website, in some situations it doesn't make sense to zoom in on a logo or icon. On the other hand, it may make sense to enable users

The bottom line is, page zoom is helpful for users, but it is not a silver bullet for developers.

to scale only the content area or certain layout elements, which would be impossible with the browser's zoom. And of course, all of the shortcomings of the pixel-based layout, including the horizontal scroll bar and excessive white space, still hold. The bottom line is, page zoom is helpful for users, but it is not a silver bullet for developers.

Hybrid Layouts

In practice, designers usually try to come up with the right mix of fixed-width, liquid and elastic layout elements to offer users the advantages of each, while minimizing the shortcomings of each as much as possible.

For instance, it has become a common practice to use em units for the content area (thus ensuring optimal line length and text scaling in Internet Explorer 6) and pixel units for the sidebar (because the sidebar often contains fixed-size ad banners that make this solution sensible). Another related technique is to have a fluid content area with "min-width" and "max-width" CSS attributes instead of the elastic element, making it possible for users to adjust the line length of the content block according to their personal preferences.

Less popular, yet still interesting, is the Jello-liquid layout ("Jello: A Different Liquid Layout", *uwmike.com*). This technique is intended to slow down the proportional growth of a flexible layout so that its content area doesn't become unusable. So, a fluid layout that has a width of 960 pixels when viewed in a browser whose view port is 1024 × 768 (960 ÷ 1024 = 0.9375) would not have a width of 1350 pixels when viewed in a browser whose view port is 1440 × 900 (1440 ÷ 1350 = 0.9375), but would have a smaller width instead. To achieve this effect, a large portion of the layout is fixed using pixel units, while the rest is defined with percentage values relative to the view port's width. The smaller the fixed portion of the layout, the better the layout stretches with the growing view port: simple and clever.

The smaller the fixed portion of the layout, the better the layout stretches with the growing view port: simple and clever.

Another interesting approach is the fluid elastic layout, which combines both liquid and elastic elements. The idea here is to set "min-width" and "max-width" for an em-based layout in percentage units (in essence, giving you the ability to limit rescaling to a certain extent by taking into account the view port's size). By setting maximum and minimum widths, the text scales to a certain point and then stops. The layout remains fluid because it automatically adapts to the user's view port, yet it is also elastic because the width of the columns is "scaled" automatically when the browser window is resized or the font size changes.

In the following example, we set the "max-width" CSS property for the container and columns. This limits the scaling of the layout to 100% of the browser's view port. Again, "max-width" is not supported in older versions of IE, so we have to implement a workaround for IE 6 and below (not shown in the following example).

```
#container {

    width: 60em;

    max-width: 100%;

}

#header {

    background-color: #cccccc;

    width:60em;

    max-width:100%;

}

#leftCol {

    width:37.5em;

    float:left;

    display: inline; /* IE 5/6 Doubled Float-Margin Bug */
```

```
   max-width:62.5%;

}

#rightCol {

   width:22.5em;

   float:right;

   max-width:37.5%;

}

#footer {

   width:60em;

   max-width:100%;

   clear:both;

}
```

Which Layout Is Right For Your Website?

The question of optimal layout doesn't have a single answer. Depending on the context, time constraints and designer's skills, each layout type has its purpose. A fixed-width approach usually works best for advanced visual layouts with heavy graphics (such as for entertainment, promotional and Flash-based websites, but sometimes also portfolios) because the images can be positioned more precisely, resulting in a more predictable and less error-prone design. Designers of such layouts need to consider the profile of the average user to make sure that the layout's width is not too narrow or wide but remains usable across various browser view ports. Coding fixed-width layouts is also more straightforward and intuitive, as one doesn't need to consider the relationship and proportions between elements.

> The question of optimal layout doesn't have a single answer. Depending on the context, time constraints and designer's skills, each layout type has its purpose.

While some designers strive for cross-browser pixel perfection, proponents of fluid designs do not think that layouts have to look identical across all platforms and screen resolutions. If this reflects your point of view, you may want to consider fluid layouts for your designs. These layouts are more time-consuming and less straightforward to develop, and they can create a risky and unpredictable environment, but they allow users to adjust layouts to their personal preferences. Liquid layouts usually have higher production costs but significantly lower maintenance costs than fixed-width layouts, and so provide a solid foundation for flexible, cross-resolution websites. Designers need to make sure that content blocks have the proper line length and should use the "min-width" and max-width" CSS properties if necessary.

While some designers strive for cross-browser pixel perfection, proponents of fluid designs do not think that layouts have to look identical across all platforms and screen resolutions.

Still can't decide? An elastic or partially elastic design is another option. When implemented correctly, elastic layouts bring a more predictable yet still flexible quality to layouts. Because elastic elements depend on font size (and not the browser's view port), they allow designers to "freeze" proportions between layout blocks, ensuring balance between elements and good readability. In particular, because optimal readability (while also important in fixed-width layouts) is more critical on text-heavy websites, flexible layouts are more often used for magazines, online shops, blogs and the like. A smart use of the fluid grid can create an adaptable layout whose proportions remain faithful to the classic rules of graphic design.

In practice, designers often create an elastic layout when they use ems for typography and containers and a smart mix of percentages and pixel widths for the rest of the layout elements. These and similar hybrid layouts are most widely used in practice, reflecting designers' attempts to find the best solution for each situation.

To conclude, it's worth mentioning that with mobile phones, netbooks and game consoles becoming viable alternatives for Web browsing, smaller (and also bigger) resolutions are becoming more important and need to be carefully considered. For such platforms, dynamic resolution-dependent techniques may turn out to be useful and even necessary extensions to your layout type of choice. Adaptive layouts, though requiring more time to create, can handle unusually small or large screen resolutions with a bit of manual customization, helping the designer deliver the most preferred results to the most users. With the growing variety of screen widths, it's only a matter of time before these techniques become essential. ■

Alessandro
Cattaneo,
Yves Peters
and
Jon Tan

Web typography:

Rules,
Guidelines
and
Common Mistakes

Typography is the soul of design; it lies at the heart of visual literacy. This chapter explores typography for the Web and describes the methods and techniques of composition that bring documents to life and facilitate understanding.

"Typography exists to honor the content", says Robert Bringhurst, author of the well-known typographic bible *The Elements of Typographic Style*. Web typography in particular entails the selection, arrangement and setting of type on the Web to enrich the meaning of text and to provide a framework upon which text can come to life. A good starting point but surely not an exhaustive definition.

Typography involves a wide range of topics and applications, even more so now with the digitization of information on the Web. It is not only about choosing the best font family, but about bringing value to communication, improving legibility, defining a brand and corporate image, selling products and making information better understood by the audience. Inadequately applying some of the common rules of typography is sometimes enough to make readers turn the other way.

Looking back to the dawn of typography, the black-letter typeface that Gutenberg used in 1455 may not be to everyone's taste today, but it was no doubt beautifully crafted and set even by today's standards. When designing for the Web, our lines cannot be so delicate, and our ligatures cannot quite be like the ones Gutenberg did on paper and vellum almost 400 years ago.

Design production methods have changed, but on the Web they've changed most dramatically of all. Typesetting is no longer manual labor performed by dedicated professionals, but is rather abstracted through code commands according to a virtual model set by designers. Type is not printed on paper anymore; it's rasterized into pixels and rendered on the screen. This is what makes Web typography different. Instead of specifying the paper or material to print on, we have to deal with a multitude of screen types, resolutions, browsers and operating systems (many of which have different rendering engines): Web typography must work on all of them.

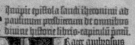

First page of the first volume of the Gutenberg Bible, printed with an early texture typeface around 1455. The decorative colored initials were hand-lettered separately by a scribe.

These days, a multitude of fonts are available at the click of a button. That's not to say they're all suitable for the Web. Most are optimized for print, not for the relatively low-resolution screens we browse the Web with. The availability of professionally created fonts for the screen and the need for consistency across platforms and browsers has put us in a position similar to that of designers and printers of yesteryear. We can use only a handful of fonts, and we've gotten to know them intimately and sometimes, with the help of a little CSS styling, we stretch them as far as they can go.

Web design evolved alongside but separately from desktop publishing – it is more embryonic; much is missing, but much we already have. We can do good work with existing tools such as HTML and CSS (and JavaScript and Flash if absolutely necessary). Some of the old rules and guidelines of typography apply to the Web, but not all. Online communication is a new and different medium through which editors and readers can interact, and this affects typography and typesetting.

Typography and Web Typography

We often consider writing a simple activity. We often think that correcting grammar, deciding the order of items in a page's layout and choosing a legible font is sufficient. But the art of typography involves several factors that are too often overlooked, especially on the Web, where the process of writing and publishing is immersive and the quality of text is often neglected. In this chapter, we will cover various typographic techniques, good practices and rules of thumb, as well as common typographic errors. But first let's take a closer look at some basic concepts of Web typography.

Legibility is affected by typeface design, screen optimization and microtypography. It has to do with the ease with which individual characters, letters or glyphs are distinguishable from one another. We can't change how established typefaces look, but we can select the right one and set it accordingly. When it comes to legibility, many designers agree on certain conventions, heuristics and typographic techniques. For instance, uppercase letters are considered more difficult to scan than lowercase letters, while regular type is more legible than italics. Good contrast between the body copy and background increases legibility, as does an appropriate line length and line height. The upper half of letters are relied on more for scanning than the lower half, while the height of ascenders and descenders

A specimen of roman typefaces by William Caslon, a famous English designer of typefaces, 18th century.

play an important role in the reader's recognition of letters. Many consider serifs more legible for this reason. As you see, when it comes to legibility, many variables come into play.

Readability is our chief concern as designers. It is influenced by layout, the placement of blocks of content and the presentation of individual items. We can do many things to ensure readability, many of which are influenced by reader's behavior. Fundamentally, people "read" the Web differently than printed material. Understanding and designing for this behavior – which is the point of user experience design – is crucial. Web typography brings key considerations.

For some designers, Web design is all about typography. On Dustin Curtis' website, the typography is prominent and dominates the design, supported by subtle visual cues.

Measure (line length) is the length of individual lines of text. The optimal length will depend on the context, but somewhere between 45 and 75 characters (including punctuation and spaces) is recommended for substantial blocks of text set flush left, ragged right. 66 characters is regarded as optimal: this line length allows for comfortable reading and doesn't require the eye to travel too far from the end of one line to the beginning of the next. One shouldn't make lines too short, either, because having to jump too frequently to the next line tires out the eye as well.

Trentwalton.com, a memorable typography-conscious blog design by Trent Walton.

Surprisingly, our recent study of typographic design patterns[1] shows that, in practice, popular text-heavy and typography-related websites (newspapers, magazines, typography-related blogs, etc.) have a longer measure, the most popular range being between 70 and 100 characters (the maximal number of characters per line). Overall, between 75 and 85 characters are displayed per line on average. Unfortunately, there are no studies that indicate whether this longer measure results in worse or better readability.

Additionally, many websites have multiple columns. Line lengths in multi-column layouts can be shorter. Traditionally,

1 http://www.smashingmagazine.com/?p=8182

justified text should be at the lower end of the range; but without precise control over word spacing and hyphenation, longer lines often yield better results in Web browsers.

While getting the measure right is important, readability can significantly improve with the right **leading (line height)**. Leading is the vertical space of an individual line of text. It is the space between two consecutive lines of text or, in other words, the distance between the baselines of two lines of text. To prevent descenders on one line from overlapping ascenders on the next, giving type generous leading is often necessary. By default, browsers set a line height of 1 em, or 1 × font size, which is often too small to be legible. A widely accepted rule of thumb is to set the leading at 1.5 × font size for paragraphs. In fact, the average line height in our study proved that this convention is still widely adopted (the average line height was 1.48 × font size). As a simple guide, the longer the measure, the greater the leading should be.

Notice that in CSS you can define line-height's value using a unit-less integer. This number acts as a scaling factor which is related to the size of the type and makes sure that the line-height is also scaled when text is resized. In general, sans serif type requires more leading then serif type and headers require less leading than blocks of text; also, darker typefaces often need more leading than lighter ones.

Tracking (letter spacing), the space between letters, or the density of blocks of text, can also be adjusted relative to the measure. Adjusting the tracking with sub-pixel values in an environment with as low a resolution as the Web is problematic because it can lead to inconsistent results. Because of this, tracking is often applied to highlight sub-headings. However, as a simple guide, if the measure is longer, and you've adjusted word spacing, an increase in letter spacing can ordinarily be justified. Approach this carefully. Pairs of characters in certain serifed typefaces can sometimes overlap. They should really be set as ligatures.

When experimenting with tracking, make sure that "AV", "ft" and "co" are clearly readable, and check that "vv" and "w" are distinguishable: the smallest inaccuracy can make text completely unreadable.

The negative letter spacing of pairs of characters is also called **kerning**; it may be necessary to adjust character pairs such as "ff", "fl" and "ffl" that actually should be set as ligatures. In some situations, kerning may be useful for improving the appearance of type; for instance, to move a "T" and small "e" closer together.

Word spacing can be adjusted relative to the measure and line height. Shorter lines warrant less word spacing. Longer lines often benefit from more word spacing, especially if they have a generous line height.

Typographic color is not pigmentation or hue, but rather the consistency of glyphs on the page. A block of text should have a uniform tone if you squint and look at it on the screen. Nothing should jump out. If it does, then reading the text will be interrupted and the flow broken. This should only be done deliberately to call attention to something. Color can also be affected by kerning. Unfortunately, nowadays this cannot be adjusted because browsers do not properly support it.

General Typographic Terms

Here is a brief overview of typography-related terms[2], so that we have a common understanding going into subsequent sections of this article.

Accent
A diacritical mark near or through a letter, indicating a variation in pronunciation. E.g. ç, à, ò, é, Å.

An overview of typography-related terms, adapted from Wikipedia.de.

2   This overview is partly based on TypeNow Glossary (http://www.typenow.net/glossary.htm)

Axis
The real or imaginary straight line on which a letterform rotates.

Baseline
The imaginary line upon which the letters in a font appear to rest.

Bowl
The generally round or elliptical forms that are the basic body shape of such letters as (uppercase) C, G, O, and (lowercase) b, c, e, o, p. Similar to the space known as an "eye".

Cap height
The height of the uppercase letters.

Counter
The white space enclosed by a letterform, whether wholly enclosed (as in "d" and "o") or partially (as in "c" and "m").

Crossbar
Horizontal stroke that connects two strokes in capital letters, such as "A" and "H".

Drop Cap
A large initial capital in a paragraph that extends through several lines.

Flush left
Setting lines of text so that any extra space is on the right and the text is against the left margin. Also called ragged right.

Flush right
Setting lines of text so that any extra space is on the left and the text is against the right margin.

Glyph
Every character in a typeface (e.g. G, $, ?, 7) is represented by a glyph. A typeface may contain more than one glyph for each character. These are usually referred to as alternates.

Ligature
Two or more letters tied as a single character to define their spatial interaction.

Majuscule
A capital (or other large) letter.

Sans serif
A typeface without serifs.

Serif
The small stroke at the end of the main strokes of letterforms. Typefaces with serifs are called serif typefaces, and those without are sans serif typefaces.

Small Caps
Small caps are capital letters but not at their full height. Many applications can create small caps by scaling down capital letters, but these false small caps lack the proper weight and proportions. A true small cap typeface retains the appropriate weight but renders the character at a smaller size.

Terminal
The end of a stroke that does not include a serif.

x-height
The height of the lowercase letters, typically exemplified by the letter x.

In practice, people often use "typeface" and "font" interchangeably. However, typeface refers to the design of a particular face, whereas font refers to the file that contains the glyphs we use. For example, Georgia is a typeface. Georgia-Bold.ttf is a font; a file containing the bold version of that typeface. In other words, the physical embodiment of a collection of letters, numbers, symbols and so on (whether it's a case of metal pieces or a computer file) is a "font" (the file you select and use).

When referring to the design of the collection (the way it looks), we speak of "typeface". As an analogy, you play an *MP3 file*, but you find the *song* beautiful.

Relative and Absolute font size units

Probably the most distinctive feature of digital type setting is the users ability to adjust **font size** to their personal preference. When selecting a font size, Web developers can use either absolute or relative units, setting either with CSS. In general, absolute units fit print design better, and using them to set type on the Web is not good practice. The only exception is for print style sheets, where absolute units can help define the dimensions of design blocks on a sheet of paper. Supported size units are pt, pc, cm, mm and in; but the keywords xx-small, x-small, small, medium, large, x-large and xx-large are options as well.

Setting an "absolute" font size does not mean that users cannot increase or decrease the font size; modern browsers allow for extensive text manipulation. Rather, the unit makes it impossible for designers to set a proportion between a parent and child element that would remain even after the font size is manually increased or decreased by the user. Hence, the "absolute" property relates to the way the element is defined in the style sheet, not to the way it is displayed on the screen.

Setting an "absolute" font size does not mean that users cannot increase or decrease the font size.

By default, modern Web browsers use a font size of 16 pixels for the <body> element: this is the value used if you don't explicitly specify any other value for the <body> element in your style sheet. To avoid complicated calculations, Richard Rutter suggested setting the <body> font size to 62.5%, which reduces the size of the text to 16px × 0.625 = 10px. Consequently, when setting the size of a headline to 18px, using 1.8em instead of 1.125em (18px : 16px = 1.125) is more convenient.

In practice, font size is usually set using relative units such as px, em or %. Pixels relate to the resolution of the display. The greater the resolution, the higher the density of pixels. Ordinarily that means smaller text.

An "em" is a unit of measurement defined as the point size of the font you are using[3].

---

3   Originally, em was said to be equal to the width of a capital "M" in a particular typeface, as the "M" was commonly cast the full-width of the square "blocks" in printing presses. However, in modern typefaces, the character M is usually somewhat less than one em wide. Besides, since some character sets do not include a capital "M", such as Chinese and the Arabic alphabet, today em generally means the height of a font in question.

It stands for the distance between baselines when the typeface is set solid (without leading). Ems are a relative unit and act as multipliers based on the text element's parent element. So, 1 em in a 16 point typeface is 16 points. If the user's browser has a default font size value of 16 pixels, then 1 em would be 16 pixels, which is essentially just a property of the currently displayed text. If the user decreases the font size to 14 pixels, then 2 em would be 2 × 14px = 28px.

The advantage of using em units for font size is the unit's native ability to set the proportion between a parent and child element and take advantage of CSS inheritance where the child of an element "inherits" the size of the parent unless explicitly changed. For instance, if the default font size is 16 pixels, and the <body> element has a font size of 2 em and the header inside the <body> tag has a font size of 1.5 em, then the font size of the header would be 1.5 × the font size of the <body> element, which is 1.5 × 2 × 16px = 48px.

To some extent, percentage values are similar to em values: the root of the document, inheritance and the relation between a parent and child element in CSS define the font size of every element. So, in the example above, one could also define the font size of the <body> element as 200% and the font size of the header as 150%; the result would be the same (48px).

In some situations the min-width and max-width properties set with ems or percentages can be very helpful in ensuring a readable measure. Usually, characters average about two-thirds of an em in length. Therefore, between 30 and 50 ems can be seen as an ideal line length.

> Because Internet Explorer 6 does not allow users to scale text set in pixels up or down, em or percentage values are recommended.

Because Internet Explorer 6 does not allow users to scale text set in pixels up or down, em or percentage values are recommended. Be careful, though, when using relative units to set type; use some kind of scale or hierarchy (see the section below) to make sure that text elements of various weights are presented accurately and appropriately.

Other relative units are rarely used in practice: although widely supported, neither "ex" nor the keywords "smaller" and "larger" (which decrease and increase the font size by 1.2 em) are used much in style sheets. Again, points (pt) are useful in print stylesheets, but shouldn't be used for the screen. People's browser may have slightly different default settings, which can result in unwelcome typographic side effects. To ensure a browser-independent presentation of text, use a CSS global reset that allows you to set type and design all elements of a website in a safe browser-independent environment. There are many kinds of CSS reset style sheets, varying from * { padding: 0; margin: 0: } to quite lengthy ones, such as Eric Meyer's Reset Stylesheet[4].

White Space Is Good Space

The importance of white space in Web typography can hardly be underestimated. Empty space makes it possible for the body copy to breathe and helps the reader absorb the information being conveyed. White space, also

The attention to typographic detail, in particular the white space, on Elliot Jay Stocks' portfolio is remarkable. Notice the balanced use of active white space to emphasize the block quote and the passive white space in the paragraph.

4 http://meyerweb.com/eric/thoughts/2007/05/01/reset-reloaded/

called "negative space", is the space between elements in a composition, or the portions of a design that are left unmarked: the space between graphics, margins, gutters and columns (macro white space), as well as between lines of text, words and image captions (micro white space). Of course, white space doesn't have to be white – the term comes from the graphic print design field, where white paper is usually used.

The white space that leads a reader from one element to another, organizes the composition and helps structure information is called "active white space". White space that regulates a block of text as a unit is called "passive white space".

In practice, many legibility issues and usability problems can be resolved or at least mitigated by a judicious, balanced use of white space. Just a couple of extra pixels of gutter, padding, margin, measure or leading can have a huge impact on the overall legibility of content. Furthermore, indenting quotes, images and lists not only can enhance the layout' s structure and presentation but can lend your design more dynamism and expressiveness.

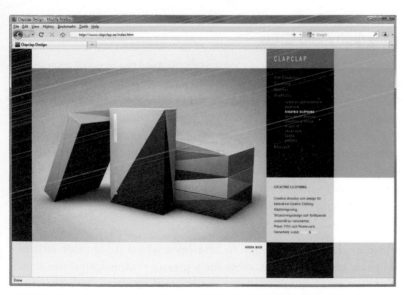

On ClapClap's portfolio website, white space dominates. It highlights the quality of the products shown and gives them more prominence and personality.

Without a good balance between the content and empty space surrounding it, text is more difficult to read and scan, leaving readers frustrated and unsure of your message. This is especially true on the Web, where many designers fill in the space "above the fold" in an attempt to grab the user's attention. These websites as a result become cluttered and hardly usable, which certainly could not have been the ultimate goal of the designers. From the user's perspective, white space provides the cues and anchors that contribute to an intuitive, pleasurable reading experience.

Some designers claim that a design can never have too much white space. This is not always the case, as the consistency and cohesion of text blocks is necessary for a balanced composition. Balancing positive (or non-white) and negative space is key to creating a beautiful, harmonized and aesthetically pleasing composition. As Mark Boulton states in one of his articles[5], "once you know how to design and manipulate the space outside, inside, and around your content, you'll be able to give your readers a head start, position products more precisely, and perhaps even begin to see your own content in a new light".

Typography and Grids

A typographic grid is a two-dimensional structure made up of a series of intersecting vertical and horizontal axes used to structure content. When used properly, the grid can serve as an armature on which a designer can organize text and images in a rational, intuitive, natural manner. It is an invisible soul that gives rhythm, order and coherence and is often used by designers to better anticipate where information should be placed, to rationalize the creative momentum. Grids are also often used in situations when graphic elements must be combined in a rapid and orderly way. At its core, the grid is the most vivid manifestation of the will to order in graphic design.

Instead of relying on intuition to determine where design elements or text *could* be placed, grids allow for a precise mathematical positioning of elements within a rigid two-dimensional structure, answering the

5   http://www.alistapart.com/articles/whitespace/

Blueprint is one of many CSS frameworks that make it easier for designers to develop websites using grids. Alternatives are Typogridphy (based on 960.gs), YUI Grids and YAML.

question of where design elements or text *should* be placed. Grids, most Web designers claim, come as *a priori*, before the content. The challenge is to find the right balance between the grid on which the content will be built and the main characteristics of the content. Some say grids stifle creativity, while others see them as a powerful framework that pushes designers towards perfectionism and precise, accurate designs.

When developing grid-based designs, designers usually start with a blank canvas or blank sheet of paper. Searching for an appropriate grid, they then use general composition rules and formulas (such as the Golden Ratio, Rules of Thirds, etc.) to subdivide the paper sheet into harmonic sections and choose inherently satisfying page and column proportions. Finally, they experiment with margins to create a perfect, dynamic typographic structure. What remains then is to flesh out the structure with content, restricting design decisions to the strict rules embodied in the grid.

Interestingly enough, as Mark Boulton states in his article "Five simple steps to designing grid systems[6]", "such an approach suggests that things which are designed to be beautiful are inherently more usable as a result" (also known as the *Aesthetic Usability Effect*). A balanced composition is naturally more aesthetically pleasing and so more usable and conducive to communication between you and your readers.

The Golden Ratio is probably one of the most popular means of laying out a grid. To comfort your visitors with a pleasing and intuitive composition, consider using when subdividing the paper sheet. Golden Ratio is the proportion of 1.618033988749895 ≈ 1.618 that holds between objects placed in relation to each other. The power of this ratio is that it can be found almost everywhere in the universe.

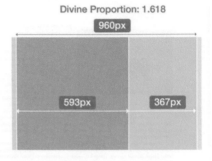

960px : 1.618 = 593px
960px - 593px = 367px

Applying divine proportion to the composition of a layout.

Consider the above example. You would like to create a fixed-width layout. The width of your layout is 960 pixels. You want a large block for your content (<content>) and a smaller block for your sidebar (<aside>). How do you calculate the widths of your columns?

- First, calculate the width of your <content> block. Make sure the ratio between this block and the layout's overall width is 1.62. Hence, you divide 960px by 1.62, which equals approximately 593px.
- Subtract 593px from the layout's overall width (960px) and you get 960px − 593px = 367px.

6 http://www.markboulton.co.uk/journal/comments/simple_steps_to_designing_grids/

- Now, if you calculate the ratio between the <content> block and the <aside> block (593px : 367px ≈ 1.615) and the ratio between the container's width and the content block's width (960px : 593px ≈ 1.618), you will have found more or less the same ratio.

This is the whole idea behind the Golden Ratio. The same holds true for fluid and elastic layouts, too.

Of course, you do not *have* to follow the Golden Ratio. What counts in the end is the result, which should be a consistent, coherent structure. The Golden Ratio is just one way to achieve it. Another option is fluid grid layouts, which are discussed in the chapter on layouts.

With and without grids: a beautiful grid-based design, with a focus on typography; created by Mark Boulton and Khoi Vinh for the presentation "Grids are Good" (http://www.subtraction.com/2007/03/18/oh-yeeaahh)

Vertical Rhythm

As the typographer Robert Bringhurst once said, "space in typography is like time in music. It is infinitely divisible, but a few proportional intervals can be much more useful than a limitless choice of arbitrary quantities". In music, a regular use of time is rhythm; in typography and Web design, a regular use of space leads us to grid theory and to vertical rhythm. Just as harmony in music can be achieved only in certain proportional time intervals, harmony in typography can be achieved only in certain proportional space intervals.

Vertical rhythm in Wilson Miner's article "Setting Type on the Web to a Baseline Grid[7]".

To understand the concept of vertical rhythm, imagine a classic exercise book with lined sheets of paper. The lines (also called baselines) are spaced equidistant from each other. If the text "sits" perfectly on the baselines, meaning that the baseline of every row of text perfectly meets the baseline of the row it is placed on, then one could say the design has a consistent vertical balance. This applies not only to the main content, but to headings, footnotes and marginal notes. Now, if you put the lined sheet of paper beneath your layout and use it as an invisible style guide to set text, you achieve vertical rhythm in your layout. Obviously, text set to a vertical rhythm is easier to scan and read because intuitively it seems to be "sitting" in the right place.

A key for maintaining vertical rhythm is leading or, put differently, the distance between two baselines. In CSS, the line-height property basically sets up the grid in the entire flow of text, giving invisible hints to readers so that

7 http://www.alistapart.com/articles/settingtypeontheweb/

they can follow a smooth regular path. Because vertical rhythm relates to the font size of text, using relative em values for the line height is natural. A nice side-effect is that the balance of the page layout is manifested in the design, regardless of the font size, style or family used.

To maintain vertical rhythm in CSS, the spacing between elements and line spacing need to equal the size of the baseline grid. For example, if you are using an 18-pixel baseline grid, meaning that there are 18 pixels between every pair of baselines, then the line spacing should be set to 18 pixels as well. And the spacing between each paragraph should also be set to 18 pixels. Here is an example:

```
body {

font-family: Arial, sans-serif;

font-size: 0.625em;

/* The font-size is now 0.625 × 16px = 10px. */

line-height: 1.8em;

/* The leading is now 18 pixels. */

}
```

For instance, if you wanted to separate paragraphs with an empty line, you would need to define an appropriate margin that is (of course) as tall as the baseline; otherwise, the paragraph would not sit in the right place:

```
p {margin-bottom: 1.5em; }
```

Of course, you can experiment with vertical space to enhance page dynamics and make the text flow less predictable. However, every variation should be defined with vertical rhythm in mind and be based on leading. Also, other text elements (headings, footnotes, images, image captions, etc.) should always relate to the basic leading with the multiplied factor, defined by the line height's value. This relation can be expressed in the following formula:

basic line-height ÷ heading font size = heading line height

Notice that creating a background image with your grid lines to be used during development can be a big help. In practice, vertical rhythm is not always possible, in particular when dealing with many images of various sizes; however, it's still an admirable goal, and getting most of the way there will still be a dramatic improvement to your page.

Typographic scale

Traditional typographic scale.

Hierarchy and Scale

Every typographic layout needs hierarchy. At its core, hierarchy supports legibility by providing clear visual clues about the structure and organization of the text. Hierarchy defines how content is to be read through. It shows the user where to start reading and where to break. It differentiates headers from body text. Although text box color can be used to give headers and body text contrast, hierarchy shows the difference in size between these elements. Hierarchy plays a huge part in making a layout scannable and is an important technique for making Web typography readable. As Jeff Croft states in his presentation "Elegant Web Typography", traditionally-set type is composed with a scale. It's useful to understand that the relationships between different sizes of type within a composition are meaningful. To achieve good hierarchy in your type setting, always compose with a scale, whether it's the traditional scale

6, 7, 8, 9, 10, 11, 12, 14, 16, 18, 21, 24, 36, 48, 60, 72

or one you thoughtfully created on your own. A scale creates harmony and cohesion in the text. Alternatively, some designers prefer to use one of the Fibonacci sequences (e.g. **16 – 24 – 40 – 64 – 104**) when defining the font size of headings and body copy[8].

8 The Fibonacci sequence is a spiral of increase where the sum of each pair creates the next ascending number in the series: 16 + 24 = 40; 24 + 40 = 64 etc. Because Fibonacci sequences help designers to achieve the Divine proportion, they are often applied for a more aesthetically pleasing design and composition.

An example of a simple typographic scale defined in CSS would be as follows:

```
body {

font-size: 0.625em;

/* Because the browser's default font size is 16 pixels, we
have now reduced the body font size to 10 pixels, which is
easier for calculations. */

}
```

AIGA achieves a beautiful, clean and intuitive hierarchy through a subtle use of color, font size and leading.

```
p  { font-size: 1.4em; /* 14px */ }
h1 { font-size: 4.8em; /* 48px */ }
h2 { font-size: 3.6em; /* 36px */ }
h3 { font-size: 2.4em; /* 24px */ }
h4 { font-size: 2.1em; /* 21px */ }
h5 { font-size: 1.8em; /* 18px */ }
h6 { font-size: 1.6em; /* 16px */ }
```

Of course, to create a proper typographic hierarchy in your design, you don't have to restrict yourself to working with font size alone; you can use color, letter style (e.g. drop caps, capitals, small-caps), italics and other options to cue readers to the structure of the content and relative weight of the text blocks on the page (see screenshot of AIGA's website above).

Paragraph Styling

Paragraphs are punctuation, the punctuation of ideas. Typographers use such layout techniques as single-line boundaries, indents, pilcrows or other ornaments, outdents and versals (e.g. drop-caps) to punctuate paragraphs in a stream of discourse.

The single-line boundary is the most common paragraph delimiter used on the Web today and the most common browser default style. Generally, the indent is still the most prevalent paragraph delimiter in printed books and publications. In some ways, the block and indent conventions exemplify the divide between Web and print. Printing cost is still a consideration, but on the Web that cost is no longer a factor. After all, usability is the only standard by which Web typography is measured.

If you use the indent, convention suggests that paragraphs that follow a heading or sub-heading should not be indented.

If you use the indent, convention suggests that paragraphs that follow a heading or sub-heading should not be indented. Tradition also suggests there should be no indent following elements such as lists and block quotes. You can achieve this without extraneous markup using adjacent sibling selectors. For example, if you have already set an indent on your paragraphs...

```
p { text-indent: 2.5em;  }
```

... then, to eliminate the indent for any paragraphs following an h1 to h3 heading, you can set:

```
h1 + p, h2 + p, h3 + p { text-indent: 0; }
```

The caveat is that this should be done only if the block quotes and indents are set flush left with hanging punctuation. Robert Bringhurst suggests, "if your paragraph indent is modest, you may for consistency's sake want to use the same indent for quotations". The same could be said of lists on the Web. In both cases, a boundary is required to separate the list or block quote from the surrounding paragraphs.

All browsers support basic paragraph styles well. However, complex treatment of versals and openings can be problematic. Some browsers still do not have mature support for such techniques as pseudo-elements

4. One em indent with boundary

Much of the material for this volume was collected during the time that I was preparing for the press the Evolution of Woman, or while searching for data bearing on the subject of sex-specialization. While preparing that book for publication, it was my intention to include within it this branch of my investigation, but wishing to obtain certain facts relative to the foundations of religious belief and worship which were not accessible at that time, and knowing that considerable labor and patience would be required in securing these facts, I decided to publish the first part of the work, withholding for the time being that portion of it pertaining especially to the development of the God-idea.

As mankind construct their own gods, or as the prevailing ideas of the unknowable reflect the inner consciousness of human beings, a trustworthy history of the growth of religions must correspond to the processes involved in the mental, moral, and social development of the individual and the nation.

By means of data brought forward in these later times relative to the growth of the God-idea, it is observed that an independent chain of evidence has been produced in support of the facts recently set forth bearing upon the development of the two diverging lines of sexual demarcation. In other words, it has been found that sex is the fundamental fact not only in the operations of Nature but in the construction of a god.

In the Evolution of Woman it has been shown that the peculiar inheritance of the two sexes, female and male, is the result of the bias given to these separate lines of development during the earliest periods of sex-differentiation; and, as this division of labor was a necessary step in the evolutionary processes, the rate of progress depended outdent-caply on the subsequent adjustment of these two primary elements or forces. A comprehensive study of prehistoric records shows that in an earlier age of existence upon the earth, at a time when woman's influence was in the ascendancy over that of man, human energy was directed by the altruistic characters which originated in and have been transmitted through the female; but after the decline of woman's power, all human institutions, customs, forms, and habits of thought are seen to reflect the egoistic qualities acquired by the male.

Paragraph styling doesn't have to be boring. In this example, the first line of the first paragraph is flush left, with subsequent first lines set with a 1em indent, ragged right, and ½ lead boundary.

10. Drop cap (versal) with bold opening

Much of the material for this volume was collected during the time that I was preparing for the press the Evolution of Woman, or while searching for data bearing on the subject of sex-specialization. While preparing that book for publication, it was my intention to include within it this branch of my investigation, but wishing to obtain certain facts relative to the foundations of religious belief and worship which were not accessible at that time, and knowing that considerable labor and patience would be required in securing these facts, I decided to publish the first part of the work, withholding for the time being that portion of it pertaining especially to the development of the God-idea.

As mankind construct their own gods, or as the prevailing ideas of the unknowable reflect the inner consciousness of human beings, a trustworthy history of the growth of religions must correspond to the processes involved in the mental, moral, and social development of the individual and the nation.

By means of data brought forward in these later times relative to the growth of the God-idea, it is observed that an independent chain of evidence has been produced in support of the facts recently set forth bearing upon the development of the two diverging lines of sexual demarcation. In other words, it has been found that sex is the fundamental fact not only in the operations of Nature but in the construction of a god.

In the Evolution of Woman it has been shown that the peculiar inheritance of the two sexes, female and male, is the result of the bias given to these separate lines of development during the earliest periods of sex-differentiation; and, as this division of labor was a necessary step in the evolutionary processes, the rate of progress depended outdent-caply on the subsequent adjustment of these two primary elements or forces. A comprehensive study of prehistoric records shows that in an earlier age of existence upon the earth, at a time when woman's influence was in the ascendancy over that of man, human energy was directed by the altruistic characters which originated in and have been transmitted through the female; but after the decline of woman's power, all human institutions, customs, forms, and habits of thought are seen to reflect the egoistic qualities acquired by the male.

Drop-cap treatment here is set without any vertical correction, and paragraphs are not justified and set with no boundary.

and adjacent sibling selectors. The developer's ability to specify fonts for body copy is also limited, and inconsistent rendering across platforms and browsers persistently frustrates creativity and precision.

11. Outdent cap (versal) with bold small caps opening

MUCH OF THE MATERIAL FOR THIS VOLUME WAS COLLECTED DURING THE time that I was preparing for the press the Evolution of Woman, or while searching for data bearing on the subject of sex-specialization. While preparing that book for publication, it was my intention to include within it this branch of my investigation, but wishing to obtain certain facts relative to the foundations of religious belief and worship which were not accessible at that time, and knowing that considerable labor and patience would be required in securing these facts, I decided to publish the first part of the work, withholding for the time being that portion of it pertaining especially to the development of the God-idea.

As mankind construct their own gods, or as the prevailing ideas of the unknowable reflect the inner consciousness of human beings, a trustworthy history of the growth of religions must correspond to the processes involved in the mental, moral, and social development of the individual and the nation.

By means of data brought forward in these later times relative to the growth of the God-idea, it is observed that an independent chain of evidence has been produced in support of the facts recently set forth bearing upon the development of the two diverging lines of sexual demarcation. In other words, it has been found that sex is the fundamental fact not only in the operations of Nature but in the construction of a god.

In the Evolution of Woman it has been shown that the peculiar inheritance of the two sexes, female and male, is the result of the bias given to these separate lines of development during the earliest periods of sex-differentiation; and, as this division of labor was a necessary step in the evolutionary processes, the rate of progress depended outdent-caply on the subsequent adjustment of these two primary elements or forces. A comprehensive study of prehistoric records shows that in an earlier age of existence upon the earth, at a time when woman's influence was in the ascendancy over that of man, human energy was directed by the altruistic characters which originated in and have been transmitted through the female; but after the decline of woman's power, all human institutions, customs, forms, and habits of thought are seen to reflect the egoistic qualities acquired by the male.

In this example, the outdent cap treatment is set without any vertical correction, and paragraphs are set with a ½ lead boundary and justified.

In the article "The Paragraph in Web Typography and Design[9]" Jon Tan explores other styling techniques and presents CSS code snippets that you can apply in your designs.

Setting Type With Fonts

Probably one of the most annoying aspects of modern Web typography is the limits facing the designer who wants to create a rich and truly cross-browser, uniform typographic design. Because of the variety of operating systems coming with pre-installed system fonts, it is hardly possible to predict whether a particular font will be correctly displayed on a user's machine or will create typographic noise, making the text harder to read and the layout harder to navigate.

Of course, one can always restrict one's font choice to the so-called "Core Web fonts", the set of 10 fonts that were designed in the 1990s-2000s to serve as the standard pack of fonts for the Web. Nowadays, these fonts are installed on over 95% of machines worldwide by default and are therefore often the first choice of designers for body copy.

Andale Mono by Steve Matteson

Arial by Robin Nicolas and Patricia Saunders

Arial Black by Robin Nicholas and Patricia Saunders

Comic Sans MS by Vincent Connare

Courier New by Adrian Frutiger and Howard Kettler

Georgia by Matthew Carter

Impact by Geoffrey Lee

Times New Roman by Stanley Morison with Starling Burgess and Victor Lardent

Trebuchet MS by Vincent Connare

Verdana by Matthew Carter

Core Web fonts in an overview.

The fonts are Andale Mono (monospaced sans serif typeface), Arial (sans serif), Comic Sans MS (script), Courier New (monospaced slab serif), Georgia

9 http://jontangerine.com/silo/typography/p/

(serif), Impact (sans serif), Times New Roman (serif), Trebuchet MS (humanist sans serif), Verdana (humanist sans serif) and Webdings (dingbat).

In recent years Palatino (Mac, old-style serif), Helvetica (sans serif), Lucida Sans Unicode (sans serif), Tahoma (humanist sans serif) and Lucida Grande (humanist sans serif) have gained popularity as well.

Georgia, certain Lucida fonts, Monaco, Trebuchet and Verdana were designed specifically for the screen, the purpose being to improve the legibility of Web copy. Together with the legendary Times New Roman, the fonts Arial, Lucida, Georgia and Trebuchet work best at a font size of 26 pixels and above and make for nice-looking headings in the body copy. Verdana, Georgia, Lucida and Arial are common choices for blocks of text; however, carefully considering the leading and measure of the text is necessary in most cases; typeface alone is certainly not a silver bullet.

With Windows Vista and Microsoft Office 2007, Microsoft introduced the ClearType Font Collection 2007, which consists of six new font families pre-installed on the PC: Calibri (humanist sans serif), Cambria (serif), Candara (humanist sans serif), Consolas (monospace), Constantia (serif) and Corbel (sans serif). While not used by the majority of people, they are pre-installed now on most modern Windows-based machines and can also be installed on Macs.

Notice that many software packages automatically install extra typefaces. For example, Office 2003 installs over 100 additional fonts. Of course, not all of these fonts are particularly refined, and not all are suitable for the Web. However they still do increase your options. You may want to check Richard Rutter's "Font Matrix[10]" which lists fonts bundled with various versions of Mac and Windows, Microsoft Office and Adobe Creative Suite.

CSS Font Stacks

While your choice of "safe" fonts is quite restricted, you do not necessarily have to use only those fonts in your style sheet. Using CSS font stacks, which is a prioritized list of preferred fonts defined in the CSS font-family

10 http://24ways.org/2007/increase-your-font-stacks-with-font-matrix

attribute, you can tell the user's browser to cycle through this list until it finds a font that is installed on the user's system and then use it to display whatever text is defined by it.

Most common fonts on all systems to 4 July 2009			
Platform and font name Installed (%)		**Sample Image**	
Microsoft Sans Serif	99.64%	Sample	Image
Verdana	98.34%	Sample	Image
Arial	98.01%	Sample	Image
Arial Black	98.01%	Sample	Image
Courier New	97.84%	Sample	Image
Tahoma	97.84%	Sample	Image
Palatino Linotype	97.83%	Sample	Image
Franklin Gothic Medium	97.63%	Sample	Image
Monaco	97.62%	Sample	Image
Lucida Console	97.59%	Sample	Image
Comic Sans MS	97.55%	Sample	Image
Impact	97.55%	Sample	Image
Trebuchet MS	97.51%	Sample	Image
Courier	97.23%	Sample	Image
Helvetica	97.03%	Sample	Image
Arial	96.83%	Sample	Image
Lucida Sans Unicode	96.14%	Sample	Image
Georgia	95.98%	Sample	Image
URW Chancery L	95.86%	Sample	Image
Verdana	95.45%	Sample	Image
Sylfaen	95.39%	Sample	Image

The most common fonts on all systems, according to Codestyle.org's "Combined font survery results" from July 2009[11].

For instance, if you want to use Baskerville, you can list it together with alternative fonts in your CSS font stack:

```
body { font-family: Baskerville, Times New Roman, Times,
serif;
}
```

And if the user doesn't have Baskerville installed on his or her machine, the browser checks for the next choice, which would be Times New Roman, and then Times and then, if none of them was found, a generic serif font.

As Nathan Ford mentions in his article "Better CSS Font Stacks[11]", when selecting a font stack, you need to first carefully consider the context of the text. Certain fonts work better for body copy, while others work better for

11 http://unitinteractive.com/blog/2008/06/26/better-css-font-stacks/

headlines: consider if the text element is a headline, a heading or a para-graph first[12]. In general, a font stack should follow the common scheme of:

font-family: ideal, alternative, common, generic;

For "ideal" fonts in headings, you can explore typographic possibilities be-yond the "safe" fonts: many fonts have quite a high market penetration, so unless you pick a really unusual one, a fair portion of users will likely have it. For body copy, "ideal" can be measured by how well it fits the overall design and its readability.

"Alternative" fonts for titles and blocks of text are usually similar to ideal ones (in terms of letterform and type) but are more popular and widely installed.

A "common" font is similar in flavor to the first two but doesn't share their distinctively sophisticated features and is usually simpler and more ordinary.

Finally, the "generic" choice is the fallback that makes sure the text is dis-played in any available generic font if none of the others is installed on the user's machine.

Examples of popular font stacks for titles are:

- Baskerville, Palatino Linotype, Times, Times New Roman, serif;
- Cambria, Georgia, Times, Times New Roman, serif
- Franklin Gothic Medium, Arial Narrow Bold, Arial, sans-serif
- Futura, Century Gothic, AppleGothic, sans-serif
- Garamond, Hoefler Text, Palatino, Palatino Linotype, serif
- Geneva, Verdana, Lucida Sans, Lucida Grande, Lucida Sans Unicode, sans-serif
- Georgia, Times, Times New Roman, serif
- GillSans, Trebuchet, Calibri, sans-serif
- Helvetica, Helvetica Neue, Arial, sans-serif
- Lucida Sans, Lucida Grande, Lucida Sans Unicode, sans-serif
- Palatino, Palatino Linotype, Hoefler Text, Times, Times New Roman, serif

12 http://www.codestyle.org/css/font-family/sampler-CombinedResults.shtml

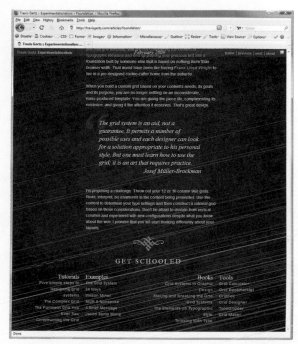

In his experiments, Travis Gertz uses various CSS font stacks to offer visitors a beautiful typographic design. In the example above, he uses Helvetica Neue for the body copy and Baskerville for dates, headings and block quotes.

- Trebuchet, Tahoma, Arial, sans-serif
- Verdana, Tahoma, Geneva, sans-serif

Here are examples of popular font stacks for body copy:

- Arial, Helvetica Neue, Helvetica, sans-serif
- Baskerville, Georgia, Cambria, Times, Times New Roman, serif;
- Cambria, Georgia, Times, Times New Roman, serif
- Century Gothic, Apple Gothic, sans-serif
- Consolas, Lucida Console, Monaco, monospace
- Courier New, Courier, monospace
- Futura, Century Gothic, AppleGothic, sans-serif
- Geneva, Lucida Sans, Lucida Grande, Lucida Sans Unicode, Verdana, sans-serif

- Georgia, Palatino, Palatino Linotype, Times, Times New Roman, serif
- GillSans, Calibri, Trebuchet, sans-serif
- Helvetica Neue, Arial, Helvetica, sans-serif
- Lucida Sans Unicode, Lucida Grande, Lucida Sans, Verdana, Arial, sans-serif
- Palatino, Palatino Linotype, Georgia, Times, Times New Roman, serif
- Times, Times New Roman, Georgia, serif
- Trebuchet, Lucida Sans Unicode, Lucida Grande, Lucida Sans, Arial, sans-serif
- Verdana, Geneva, Tahoma, sans-serif

When defining your font stack, make sure the fonts you choose are not too obscure and that even alternative and common fonts will work well in overall design. Putting very different fonts in a font stack is usually not a good idea because variations in font size, measure and leading can produce quite surprising results for the body copy and headings, even making them unreadable or breaking the layout. Finally, you need to consider the possibility of situations where, for instance, the **Careful consideration up front saves trouble down the road.** second choice in your font stack for headings is used while the third choice in your font stack for the body copy is used. Would the text flow and be readable in such a case? What about other combinations? Careful consideration up front saves trouble down the road.

Text Replacement Techniques

Although "Core Web fonts" allow for consistent, platform-independent typography, some designers prefer to experiment with unusual type settings for unconventional design solutions. Various text replacement techniques exist to replace plain text on your page with an image or movie that embeds the font of your choice and displays it to the user – in particular, if that font isn't installed on the user's machine. Such techniques often rely on client-side JavaScript support or server-side scripts that generate the images with the embedded text on the fly, while keeping content accessible and readable by most visitors.

In general, there are four kinds of text replacement techniques:

- **Static replacement with an image,** in which the designer simply replaces text with an image that has the text embedded in it, while keeping the content SEO-friendly. The Radu, Phark and Malarkey Image Replacement methods recommend large negative margins, letter spacing and text indents, respectively, to hide text and using the background property to display the image instead). Notice that using just an img element for textual content (without image replacement techniques described above) ignores the need for semantic HTML markup and therefore should be avoided.

- **Dynamic replacement with an image,** which goes beyond static image replacement and automates image generation using JavaScript (client-side) or PHP (server-side). The designer uploads the font file to the server, where it is used by the server script to generate images that replace the text. Techniques that employ this method include Scalable Inline Image Replacement, Dynamic Text Replacement, Facelift Image Replacement and Scalable Jens Image Replacement.

- **Dynamic replacement with a movie,** which relies on Flash movies that have typefaces embedded in them. These movies are called on demand whenever text needs to be replaced (using, for example, sIFR). The advantage of this technique is that text can be selected and copied. However, this technique increases page load times, and both JavaScript and Flash have to be supported by the user's browser for it to work. Despite these serious limitations in accessibility, sIFR is probably the best-known text replacement technique on the Web, with various plug-ins and third-party applications.

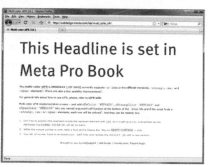

sIFR (Scalable Inman Flash Replacement) in action: Meta Pro Book is embedded in a Flash movie.

Dave Shea's experiment with Cufón: the body copy is more elegant and makes for more comfortable reading. Cufón and the @font-face attribute are currently among the most promising typographic techniques on the Web.

- **Dynamic replacement with canvas and VML**, which consists of two separate parts: a font generator, which converts fonts to a proprietary format using VML, and a rendering engine. Cufón[13], an example of this technique, does not require any plug-ins, is cross-browser-compatible and is faster than comparable techniques. Its advantage is that users can select and copy the whole text on the page and don't have to select replaced text explicitly, which is not possible with sIFR or the other techniques. Another example is Typeface.js[14].

Whichever technique you choose, make sure the content remains accessible and readable, even if Flash or JavaScript is not installed or enabled in the user's browser. Static replacement with images comes with major accessibility issues. And dynamic techniques usually increase server load and so sometimes require some sort of caching. Still, Cufón and sIFR are currently growing in popularity; and Cufón is often preferred to sIFR because it is cross-platform compatible and lightweight, even if its settings are not as flexible as sIFR's.

13 http://wiki.github.com/sorccu/cufon
14 http://typeface.neocracy.org

@font-face Attribute

Embedding fonts using text replacement techniques is often time-consuming and quirky, because designers have to embed typefaces in Flash movies or use server-side libraries to generate images with embedded typography. The drawback of these techniques is that they usually rely on the browser's JavaScript support and are quite difficult to handle in practice. Obviously, native support of typefaces using pure CSS would be a preferable and more intuitive solution. And that's exactly what the @font-face attribute of the CSS 3 Web Fonts Module is supposed to deliver.

With @font-face, embedding fonts is done in two steps. First, a new font is added to the list of available fonts in the style sheet. This is done using the @font-face property:

```
@font-face {

font-family: MuseoSans;

src: url('fonts/museo_sans.otf') format ("opentype");

font-weight: bold;
}
```

In this example, the designer declares Museo Sans as one of the available fonts to be used by the browser to render text. Then in the second step, to style a text element with the newly declared font, we use the font in our regular CSS declaration, like this:

```
h1 {

font-family: MuseoSans, Arial, sans-serif;
}
```

The browser will load the museo_sans.otf file and use it to display h1 headlines. If the browser doesn't support the @font-face property, it will simply be ignored. Note that only freely available fonts may be uploaded to the server, because the files will be accessible not only to browsers but to users, who can download the files from the server. The license agreement should explicitly state that the font may be used with the @font-face attribute.

Typekit is a simple solution that comes with a Web-only font linking license that allows you to embed commercial fonts in your layout. (Image by Andy Clark[16])

Typekit[15] or Fontdeck[16] is another option. Both services offer a simple solution that comes with a Web-only font linking license that allows you to embed commercial fonts in your layout. A font file, or certain weights in a font family, are stored on a third-party server, and the designer subscribes to Typekit to rent (not buy) the font. Upon payment, the designer is given a JavaScript file to include on the page and be used with simple CSS.

Choosing The "Right" Type

With literally more than a hundred thousand typefaces to choose from, finding the right one for a specific purpose may seem like a daunting task. The common mistake is to choose a beautiful typeface, one that looks attractive, thus favoring form over function. This is putting the cart before the horse. However strange this sounds, the "look" of the typeface should be your least concern. But if looks are not so important, what do we base our decision on? The most important criterion is the context in which the typeface will be used and the purpose it will serve.

15 http://blog.typekit.com/2009/05/27/introducing-typekit/
16 http://ilovetypography.com/2009/08/07/the-font-as-service/

Consider context and narrative

Before getting into the nitty-gritty of choosing a typeface and layout, always read the text first if possible. This may seem obvious, but the type-face and its presentation should be determined by the meaning of the text itself. There's an obvious problem, though. In the era of the Web, we often deal with two very different kinds of narratives:

Enacted narratives: the ones we know and love. The meaning and substance of the text is known by the designer beforehand. The audience starts at the beginning and reads to the end, becoming enlightened along the way.

Emergent narratives: this is content that will be generated after our design is complete. Think of social networks, in which everyone contributes text, or websites with a CMS or blog engine in which new copy is constantly generated. The audience might skim this content, jumping around the page and website in leaps and bounds, gathering nuggets of meaning along the way, pausing only when something grabs their attention.

For enacted narratives, we can read the text beforehand, understand its meaning, tone and nuances, and we can choose the type accordingly. But what do we do for emergent narratives? Well, we do the best we can. Look at the brand and environment. Imagine the context in which the text will be read. Choose a type that enriches the meaning of the text but fades into the background rather than clamors for attention.

Never climb a mountain wearing dancing shoes

Virtually every designer of typefaces creates a font with well-defined criteria and for specific functions. It is up to the website designer to recognize that function before choosing the typeface. At one end of the spectrum are the workhorse typefaces designed to perform well in small sizes and unfavorable conditions (the hiking boots), and at the other end are the display typefaces (the dancing shoes).

Workhorse typefaces have sturdy features: conventional and easily recognizable letterforms, generous letter spacing, solid serifs, clear open counters, a tall x-height and ink traps (cut-out areas that prevent corners from clogging up from spreading ink). Ink spread is a non-issue on the Web, but the other factors apply. Display typefaces are much more delicate and have considerably more leeway in their shapes. There is a world between these two extremes, and many of the typefaces at either end were designed for very specific applications. In the middle are the very important day-to-day typefaces that are fit for normal text but suitable also for headlines.

Workhorse typefaces are more flexible than display typefaces. To some extent, one can wear hiking boots to a posh reception. If you combine them with casual jeans and a stylish shirt and jacket, you might get away with

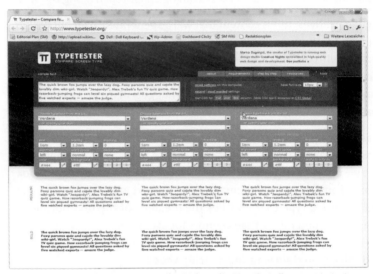

Marko Dugonjic's Typetester is a popular Web application that allows you to test different typefaces, leading and measure on the screen and choose the best one.

it, just as workhorse typefaces might look acceptable in headlines if you adapt their spacing and use them in combination with the right design elements. But you wouldn't climb a mountain in dancing shoes. Sure, you *could*, but don't come crying after. Likewise, never use display typefaces for body text.

Size *does* matter

Of course, a lot of the above has to do with type size. With the advent of scalable digital type, any font can be used at any size, and the time-honored mastering process is abandoned. As a result, many designs suffer in this age of convenience: many display fonts are too ornate or fragile to be displayed at a small size, and text fonts are clunky and dull when set large.

Although they may look similar, text and display typefaces reveal many differences when scaled up.

Optical size mastering isn't important only for print. When designing for the screen, similar problems arise. The stroke thickness to pixel size ratio is crucial. Delicate shapes break up and hairline serifs disappear when type is so small that fine lines shrink to less than a pixel wide. Fonts with a short x-height become hard to read if the body of the type is not rendered with enough pixels, as do unconventional or intricate shapes, closed counters and tightly spaced letters.

OpenType, TrueType or PostScript Type 1?

Today, digital typefaces are available in three different font formats: OpenType, PostScript Type 1 and TrueType. This can sometimes be a little confusing. Knowing if the file format of your font is compatible with the software you are going to use it in is very important.

In general, if you are using a modern image editing application, you will experience hardly any problems with the OpenType format. The two main benefits are its cross-platform compatibility – you can work with the same font file on the Mac, Windows and other computer systems – and its ability to support extended character sets and layout features. They provide rich linguistic support and advanced typographic control. Currently, all Adobe applications (InDesign, Illustrator, Photoshop etc.) provide advanced Open-Type feature support, such as automatic substitution of alternate glyphs, automatic ligatures, small capitals, swashes and old-style figures.

Note that OpenType fonts can be installed and used alongside PostScript Type 1 and TrueType fonts. Because those fonts rely on OpenType-specific tables, non-compatible applications running on systems prior to Mac OS X and MS Windows 2000 are not able to use them without system services such as ATM. And even on the newest computers and latest operating systems some programs are still lagging behind.

A PostScript Type 1 font can hold up to 256 glyphs; an OpenType font file up to 256^2 or 65,536.

PostScript Type 1
8-bit
256 available slots

OpenType (Unicode)
16-bit
35,536 available slots

What are you after: a basic meal or gourmet dining?
A typeface is more than what you see on the keyboard. In addition to the alphabet, numbers and assorted punctuation, the average font also includes a series of "hidden" characters. They can be accessed via the shift and/or option key or through special menus. The approximately 250 glyphs found in standard typefaces are sufficient for display and basic text use. However, just as you can't get away with serving a burger and fries at a fine restaurant, good typography requires quite a bit more. If you are considering a certain typeface for professional typesetting, make sure the following extra features are available.

For instance, small capitals (also called small caps) are a little taller than the x-height. They can be used for acronyms or to avoid putting words in all capitals, which stands out too much in running text. They can also be used for emphasis or for the first words or line of a chapter or paragraph. Petite caps are even smaller: exactly as high as the x-height. Some designers use them for typographic experiments like mixed-case setting (of lowercase and uppercase forms), also called unicase setting.

Standard typefaces mostly come with only one set of numerals, yet different styles are needed for professional typesetting. Proportional hanging figures blend in perfectly with running text; proportional lining figures match text in all caps; tabular figures are needed for setting tables and number crunching; and superscript and subscript figures are for setting fractions and scientific text. This last type of text requires not only superscript and subscript characters but special mathematical characters and several types of brackets as well.

When choosing an appropriate typeface, make sure to check that the font family is complete and includes all glyphs you may need in your design. For instance, some cheap font families may not include German umlauts (ä, ö, ü) or Eszett (ß).

In fact, ligatures are needed when an overhanging part of a character bumps into the next character. Most digital fonts used to include only a limited number of "f" ligatures, which was insufficient. An extended ligature set guarantees that any unusual letter combination will have an aesthetically pleasing glyph. Some designs include quite unusual ligatures, often to add some swoosh to the type. Swoosh can also be added with swash characters, be they initial capitals or initial and end characters.

Take a careful look at a typeface before purchasing it. To analyze a type family, carefully consider how the glyphs look at a big font size (100 to 150 points). Also look at how various members of the family will look in the size you will typically use them in. Are the italics readable? Are the small-caps clear enough? How do the bold and italics work together? Is it easy to read a word like "rococo"? Can you distinguish between the 0 (zero) and o (small o) in the word "lolo"? What about ligatures in the words "floria" and "Eigenschaft"?

"Don't insert too many wacky signifiers!"

The *Official Guide*
to TYPE Selection

THE UNABRIDGED VERSION 2³/₄

FEBRUARY 28th, 2009

Extended ligature set	Small caps	Lining figures
Discretionary ligatures	Swashes	Oldstyle numerals
Capital ligatures	Superscript characters	Fractions

Professional typesetting requires the presence of small caps, several sets of numerals, extended ligature sets, assorted expert glyphs, and it never hurts to have alternates and swash characters available. On the image: Capsa expert characters.

Sans or serif? ... Or monospace or cursive?

The ongoing debate about serif versus sans serif on the Web has to do with legibility. Vociferous advocates are on both sides of the argument. As screen sizes increase and resolutions or pixel density increase, the argument that less fussy sans serif forms aid legibility loses some merit. As Jost Hochuli demonstrates in *Detail in typography*, serif fonts may be easier to read, but many people's familiarity with and attachment to commonly used fonts on the Web may make these typefaces more legible anyway. However, even typefaces designed specifically for the screen can appear very different across platforms. What is highly legible on one screen may not be on another.

Here are some key factors in choosing typefaces for legibility on the screen:

Familiar letterforms. Choose a face with customary shapes. Avoid "quirky" typefaces that break convention. Never set body copy in all capitals or all small-caps, and be careful with italics and obliques and other variations of the normal shape. For example, ascenders and descenders are important for legibility; choose a font whose ascenders for letters such as "b" and "d" rise above the x-height, and vice-versa for "p" and "q".

Choose fonts that were designed for the screen. Most were not, either not being designed for the screen or not even optimized for it by the foundry. If a font is not hinted properly, screen performance will suffer. For example, the bar in the capital "A" can disappear at small sizes, as do serifs and other delicate glyph components.

True fonts, not synthetics. Consider the available fonts of the typeface you wish to use. Many common typefaces have only regular, bold, italic and bold italic fonts available. Whatever stylistic variants are available will have been specifically designed.

Browsers are able to synthesize fonts. A common example is synthetic italics or, more properly, obliques (regular type set at an angle without changing the letterform, to mimic a true oblique). The ubiquitous type-face of Apple, Lucida Grande by Charles Bigelow and Kris Holmes has no italic or oblique font. That doesn't stop people from instantiating one with CSS, though; the browser synthesizes it, and to our eyes it looks awful. Small caps is another example; none of the core Web fonts have a small-caps version. However, we use synthetic small-caps sometimes. The trick is to avoid synthetic fonts, but use your discretion and know when to do it and why.

Generous x-height. Again, this is the distance between the baseline and (typically) the top of a lowercase "x" (hence the name) compared to the overall body height. A generous x-height is critical for legibility, especially on the screen. Georgia and Verdana both were designed specifically for the screen; both have a generous x-height.

Comfortable letter spacing. It is possible to adjust letter spacing with CSS using the letter-spacing property; a font that already has good letter spacing is a great starting point.

Comfortable word spacing. This is the gap between words. It can also be adjusted with CSS but should be easy on the eye without adjustment.

A beautiful face is the one that serves its purpose

When all other requirements have been met, you can finally pick the typeface whose "looks" you like the most, the one you find most beautiful. But as you now know, this is actually the last step in the selection process. Understanding the importance of the preceding steps is vital. A typeface that truly serves its purpose will get you farther than one that is merely beautiful. Unless the font performs well on your operating system, comes in all the required languages, has a complete character set, is part of a suitably large family and has a design that evokes the right atmosphere and cultural connotations, your message could be misunderstood.

Complements will get you everywhere

Combining fonts is an art. Unless there's a very good reason to use more, fewer is always better. Many designers use the same typefaces time after time, relying on the styles within each font for variety. Even more rely on just a handful, no matter how many they download, because those few are tried and trusted friends. So it is with the Web.

We may have hundreds of thousands of typefaces at our disposal in the years to come, but with a few well-loved and well-understood families, most designers can never go wrong.

Combining serif and sans serif is a well-worn path that can work wonders. When combining them for body text, be sure to match the x-height.

Georgia Verdana

Georgia and Verdana by Matthew Carter at the same size. Verdana seems larger.

Georgia Verdana

Georgia with Verdana at a smaller size. The x-height matches. They seem comparable in size.

Just as opposite colors on the color wheel are complements, so it is with type. However, tread carefully. The contrast between certain fonts can be just as harsh as the contrast between blue and yellow.

Keep in mind that computer displays have much greater black/white contrast than the typical printed page. Therefore, many designers prefer off-black to pure black on white backgrounds[17]. Likewise, it is usually more elegant to use very light gray instead of pure white on black backgrounds. To achieve quality typography with CSS, aim for the smallest effective difference and "make all visual distinctions as subtle as possible, but still clear and effective[18]".

Try alternate styles of the same face as a starting point. Use a bold as a display face for headings, small caps or caps for sub-headings, an italic for further sub-headings and a regular for body copy. Experiment with style to find the right hierarchy of elements on the page.

If you do get a little experimental with your font stacks, beware of baseline variations between fonts on different platforms. You may think Helvetica Neue and Arial would have similar baselines but they don't. The differences in viewing a page in Windows with Arial and on OS X with Helvetica can nudge the grid alignment askew.

Pay Attention To Details

Now that we've considered key typographic concepts, terms, best practices and practical recommendations, let's look at typography from a different perspective. To achieve beautiful, well-rounded and effective typography, one needs to create properly formatted and carefully written copy. That is, if you want to leave a great impression, you need to polish your writing and pay close attention to the smallest typographic details.

Widows and orphans

A widow a paragraph-ending line that falls at the beginning of the following page/column, thus separated from the remainder of the text. An orphan is a word, part of a word, or very short line that appears by itself

17   Jeff Croft, "Elegant Web Typography"
18   Edward Tufte, "Visual Explanations"

at the end of a paragraph. Widows and orphans create awkward rags, interrupt the reader's flow and impair readability. They can be avoided by adjusting the type size, leading, measure, word spacing and letter spacing or by entering manual line breaks.

Unfortunately, there is no easy way to prevent widows and orphans with CSS. You can use a jQuery plug-in called jQWidon't or the Typogrify Word-Press plug-in which places a non-breaking space ( ) between the last two words of a text block[19].

Good

Lorem ipsum dolor sit amet, consectetur lout adipiscing elit. Integer posuere orci quis ligula. Donec egestas massa vulputate nisl. Curabitur venenatis. **dolor sit amet antetut mauris.**

Nulla ac odio. Praesent bibendum justo id posuere orci quis ligula massa vulputate

egestas massa vulputate nisl mauri. Suspendisse magna tellus, faucibus, sodales, vehicula eget.

Lorem ipsum dolor sit amet, consectetur lout adipiscing elit. Integer posuere orci quis ligula. Donec egestas massa vulputa nisl. Curabitur venenatis nullam.

Bad

Lorem ipsum dolor sit amet, consectetur lout adipiscing elit. Integer posuere orci quis ligula. Donec egestas massa atheis vulputate nisl. Curabitur venenatis aerues **mauris.**

Nulla ac odio. Praesent bibendum justo id mauris. Suspendisse magna tellus,

dapibus sodales, vehicula eget.

Lorem ipsum dolor sit amet, consectetur lout adipiscing elit. Integer posuere orci quis ligula. Donec egestas massa vulputate nisl. Curabitur venenatis. Nullam egestas facilisis antetut.

Widows and orphans are bad practice in typography.

Clean rags and hyphenation

When setting a block of text that is not justified, be sure to keep the rag (the uneven side) balanced without any sudden "holes" or awkward shapes. A bad rag can be unsettling to the eye and distract the reader. A good rag has a "soft" unevenness, with no lines that are too long or too short. There is no way to control this with CSS, so to get a good rag you must make manual adjustments to the block of text.

19 http://blog.hamstu.com/2007/05/31/web-typography-just-got-better/

Good

Lorem ipsum dolor sit amet, consectetur adipiscing elit. Integer posuere orci quis ligula. Donec egestas massa vulputate nisl. Curabitur venenatis. Nullam egestas facilisis ante. Suspendisse tincidunt. Etiam vitae leo id mauris laoreet luctus. Cum sociis natoque penatibus et magnis dis parturient montes, nascetur ridiculus mus. Nulla ac odio. Praesent bibendum justo id mauris.

Bad

Lorem ipsum dolor sit amet, consectetur adipiscing elit. Integer posuere orci quis ligula. Donec egestas massa id mauris. Curabitur venenatis. Nullam egestas facilisis ante. Suspendisse tincidunt. Etiam vitae leo id mauris laoreet luctus. Natoque penatibus et magnis dis parturient montes, nascetur ridiculus mus. Nulla ac odio.

Be sure to keep the rag (the uneven side) balanced, without any sudden "holes" or awkward shapes.

Another solution would be automatic hyphenation and justification. At the moment, though, modern browsers have a very simple hyphenation mechanism that doesn't allow for the kind of sophisticated justification we know from print design. Many variables in display environments make it impractical to hyphenate manually [for instance, using the soft hyphen (­)].

On the Web, justified text is usually more difficult to read and scan than left-aligned text. Some server-side and client-side auto-hyphenation solutions are phpHyphenator[20] and Hyphenator[21]. Keep in mind that justified text usually doesn't work as well with sans serif typefaces as with serif typefaces and it works best with a narrower measure.

Emphasis

Emphasizing words without interrupting the reader is important. Italics are widely considered to be the best form of emphasis. Other common forms of emphasis are bold, caps, small caps, type size, color and different typeface. No matter which you choose, try to limit yourself to one. Combining, say, caps, bold and italics would be disruptive and look clumsy.

20 http://yellowgreen.de/phpHyphenator
21 http://code.google.com/p/hyphenator/

Here are some different ways to emphasize with CSS (keep in mind that the font-variant style only works if the font supports the small-caps variant):

```
span {

font-style: italic;

}

h1 {

font-weight: bold;

}

h2 {

text-transform: uppercase;

}
```

Hanging punctuation

Good typographic practice is to put pull quotes, bullets and numbers outside the flow of text. Indenting bullets can disrupt the flow of text. With hanging punctuation, text and quotes are highlighted and appear more sophisticated and legible. In your CSS, make sure to hang the punctuation outside of the margin of the body text. For pull quotes, give the CSS text-indent property a negative value (which will depend, of course, on the font size).

An example of good and bad quote presentation. Hang the quotation marks outside of the margin of the body text so that the visual rhythm is not broken.

Good

" Lorem ipsum dolor sit amet, consectetur atse adipiscing elit. Integer posuere orci quis ligula. Donec egestas massa vulputate nisl. Curabitur venenatis. Nullam luoi egestas facilisis ante. "

Bad

" Lorem ipsum dolor sit amet, consectetur atse adipiscing elit. Integer posuere orci quis ligula. Donec egestas massa vulputate nisl. Curabitur venenatis. Nullam luoi egestas facilisis ante. "

```
blockquote {

    text-indent: -0.8em;

    font-size: 12px;

}
```

For the same effect with ordered (ol) or unordered (ul) lists, use the list-style-position property to push bullets outside the left rung. This technique is supported in all major browsers:

```
ul, ol {

list-style-position: outside;

}
```

Indented lists can also serve as calls to action as people skim the page. If you do use an indent, make sure you do it deliberately, for a specific purpose.

Ampersand with style

The ampersand is essentially a series of curves and demonstrates nice variation from font to font. With CSS, you may want to choose a special font for it. The Simplebits article *"Use the Best Available Ampersand[22]"* offers an interesting and effective approach to choosing the best ampersand by setting up your font family of choice.

(X) HTML:

```
<p>pixels <span class="amp">&amp;</span> text</p>
```

Simplebits has a beautiful and elegant ampersand in its slogan.

22 http://simplebits.com/notebook/2008/08/14/ampersands.html

```
CSS:

span {

font-family: Baskerville, Palatino, "Book Antiqua", serif;

font-style: italic;

}
```

Do not use a hyphen for the em dash

If you need to interrupt yourself, do it with an em dash (—) instead of a pair of hyphens (--). This is a top pet peeve of countless editors.

Do not use dumb quotes

Quote "this way" (with quotation marks that look like 66 and 99) and not "this way". Open and closed quotes are not the same. Please notice that the choice of quotes varies depending on the language in which it is used. For American English, quotes are normally surrounded by double quotation marks, while nested quotes use single quotation marks. For British English, it can be either way: doubles then singles, or singles then doubles. In CSS, you can style the appearance of quotes using the :lang pseudo-class:

```
:lang(en-us)>q {

quotes: "\201c" "\201d" "\2018" "\2019";

}

:lang(en-gb)>q {

quotes: "\2018" "\2019" "\201c" "\201d";

}
```

Modern browsers support this method of styling, so it is highly recommendable to consider regional differences when using[23] smart quotes, and avoid the so-called "dumb" quotes. For instance, in Arabic, Dutch and German language „this way" (99 and 66) is correct and in Russia, France and Italy guillemets – «this way» – are more common.

---

23 Of course, Internet Explorer, even version 8, doesn't support it, although it is aware of the element. To avoid problems with encoding quotations, adding numeric values is important.

Do not double-space between sentences

The antiquated practice of double-spacing between sentences seemed finally to be laid to rest thanks to Web typography. Just a few years ago, committing this font faux pas required manually inserting a blank ASCII space. Now, some content management systems will actually format the double-spacing for you if you let them. Don't give them the chance! Only use single spaces between sentences.

Use accent characters when necessary

Although accent characters can be difficult to type in or copy in HTML, paying attention to these non-standard characters is an important courtesy and sign of respect. Many tables listing character entities, including the one on Wikipedia[24], are available for your convenience.

Treat text as a user interface

Word choice in interfaces is extremely important and can make or break the functionality of a website. The presentation of those words is equally important. Unstyled letterforms give no indication as to what users should interact with.

Text as content   Text as UI

 cameronmoll

Title: Principal
Company: Cameron Moll Design
Location: Springville, Utah
Member Since: August 17, 2005

Designer, speaker, wannabe drummer. I spend my free time bird watching, quilting, and playing the occasional ping pong game. When faced with Sed ut perspiciatis unde omnis iste natus error sit voluptatem accusantium doloremque laudantium, totam rem aperiam, eaque ipsa quae ab illo inventore veritatis et quasi... **[read more]**

Interests: Web design, web development, media production, entrepreneurship, branding, marketing, positioning, podcasting, analytics, software development

 cameronmoll

Title: Principal
Company: Cameron Moll Design
Location: Springville, Utah
Member Since: August 17, 2005

Designer, speaker, wannabe drummer. I spend my free time bird watching, quilting, and playing the occasional ping pong game. When faced with Sed ut perspiciatis unde omnis iste natus error sit voluptatem accusantium doloremque laudantium, totam rem aperiam, eaque ipsa quae ab illo inventore veritatis et quasi... **[read more]**

Interests: Web design, web development, media production, entrepreneurship, branding, marketing, positioning, podcasting, analytics, software development

In his presentation entitled "Nine skills that separate good from great designers", Cameron Moll discusses the importance of treating text as user interface[26].

The image above compares text as content and text as user interface. On the left is unformatted text, and on the right the text functions as a user

24 http://en.wikipedia.org/wiki/List_of_XML_and_HTML_character_entity_references

interface. Notice the different colors and weights of the text, the ample spacing between paragraphs and lines and the links that stand out and are easy to identify.

If you want your content to convey a function as well as a meaning and to help your users understand how they are supposed to achieve their goal with your text, you'll have to include subtle visual cues like these.

Quotes

Quotes highlight excerpted text. They are always used for testimonials and sometimes for blog comments, but most importantly they are used in paragraphs of text. Not all quotes are the same, though. Pull quotes are short excerpts of text taken straight from the page itself. They pull a bit

Last week FontShop asked Twitter users to name their favorite underused typeface.

> *There will always be a place for classic type in contemporary design, and it's safe and easy to rely on the same old standards, but using type that is underused is often the best way to stand out in an increasingly crowded and homogeneous design landscape.*

Read more...   FILED UNDER   Typography

A vivid block quote element on ldsgn.org.

25 http://www.cameronmoll.com/archives/001266.html

of text out of the flow of content and repeat it in a prominent location on the page to grab user's attention.

Like pull quotes, block quotes (or, more precisely, block quotations) are set off from the main text as distinct paragraphs or blocks. Unlike pull quotes, they contain a passage from an external source that does not appear elsewhere on the page. Block quotations are usually set within the main flow of text. "Normal" quotes cite content from other sources and are incorporated in the main flow of content rather than set apart.

According to HTML specifications, three elements are available to semantically mark up quotations: <blockquote>, <q> and <cite>. While all mark up quotes, each is meant for a different use.

- A block quote, <blockquote>, is used for relatively long quotations; it is a large section of text set apart from the main body. This text usually comes from an external source, but can also refer to your previous article.
- <q> is used for short inline quotations:

```
<p>Andrew answered <q>fonts</q>, but Steven said

<q>typefaces</q></p>
```

Although it is rarely used, it has some useful properties. For instance, you can modify the appearance of quotations inside the <q> element using CSS. This is helpful because languages have different quotation marks (see the section "Do not use dumb quotes" above).

- Finally, <cite> defines an in-line citation or reference to another source:

```
<p>But then <cite>Andrew</cite> said <q>No, I think these

fonts work better</q>.</p>
```

Quotes, braces, lines, indendation, quote visuals, dialogue boxes, balloons – there are a number of paths a designer can take to create a beautiful and memorable quote. Design solutions vary in colors, forms and sizes. Different techniques produce different results; however, it is important that it is clear to the visitors that the quote is actually a quote, otherwise it becomes hard to keep track on the content. Also, use quotes sparingly, they should play a secondary role, supporting the main content, not the other way around. They should be a pleasant diversion, not a central design feature.

As pretty as they are, pull quotes have inherent problems in the way they are placed in the middle of HTML content. To people viewing the page in CSS-enabled browsers, all may be hunky-dory. But for those who have disabled CSS or are using screen readers, pull quotes appear slap bang in the middle of the main content. A quote suddenly appearing between two paragraphs but not connected to them will most certainly break the flow and confuse readers.

> As pretty as they are, pull quotes have inherent problems in the way they are placed in the middle of HTML content.

If your content has pull quotes, providing a little extra information for users who stumble on them is probably wise. In (X)HTML, you could include a message, hidden from view with CSS, that says "Start of pull quote" before the quote and "end quote" after it. You could even have something like the "Skip navigation" link that lets users skip the pull quote and continue with the main content.

Hyphens and special characters

Finally, here we cover some of the most common typographic symbols, their uses and good practice when dealing with advanced typography and special kinds of text.

The hyphen (-) is one of the most used typographic symbols. This punctuation mark divides and joins words. The hyphen is not a minus sign (−) or a dash (–, —, —). The soft hyphen (­) appears at the end of a line of text to indicate that a word continues on the next line. "Soft" refers to the fact that the hyphen should disappear if the entire word ends up being written on one line. The hard hyphen wraps text and joins words. "Hard" refers to the fact that the hyphen must always

> The hard hyphen wraps text and joins words.

appear, even when the hyphenated term appears on one line (*self-respect*).
Unfortunately, at the moment, hyphens have to be inserted manually in
HTML.

En dash and **em dash:** the former is longer than a hyphen and half an em
dash. It indicates a range, such as for dates, numbers, game scores and
pages (*2:00–3:00 p.m.*), or groups com-
pound adjectives (*Meyer–Stevenson Lex-*
icon). The HTML entity for the en dash
is &8211;.

An em dash is 1em wide. It indicates an
interruption in speech (*I was debugging*
the style sheet – wait a second; what was
he saying about IE6?). The HTML entity
is &8212;. Note that some dashes bene-
fit from having spaces around them; for instance, the em dash can be surrounded by a thin ( ) or hair ( ) space[26].

| - **hyphen** |
| – **en dash** |
| — **em dash** |

The hyphen, en dash and em dash.

Curly single and double opening quotes are not the correct symbols for feet
and inches. A single prime should be used to represent feet and minutes
(′ – not supported in HTML 4.01), and a **double prime** for inches
or seconds (″ – not supported in HTML 4.01).

To indicate missing words in a quotation or a thought that trails off, use an
ellipsis (…) instead of three consequent periods. Three periods are
not an ellipsis. This is a very common mistake because they look so alike,
but semantically they are different.

To recap, here is a reference table of the most common typographic symbols. Using the numeric Unicode references is good practice because non-
numericals may not be parsed properly[27] (for example, named entities are
bound to a DTD and do not always translate, so an RSS parser may have
problems with them).

---

26 See also Jon Tan's "Typographic Spaces Test Suite" http://jontangerine.com/silo/typography/
    spaces/, a series of examples of different types of typographic spaces, using the core Web fonts
    for user agent and operating system comparison.
27 http://people.w3.org/~dom/archives/2005/04/named-versus-numeric-entities/

    &   Ampersand (&): used in many different ways in regular written text, programming languages, etc.

    ©   Copyright sign (©)

    ®   Registered trademark (®)

    §   Section sign (§): when used twice, §§ means 'sections'.

    '   Apostrophe (')

    ' ' " " Quotation marks (‘ ’ “ ”)

    ×   Multiplication sign (×)

    °   Degree sign (°)

    ¼   One-quarter fraction (¼)

    ½   One-half fraction (½)

    ¾   Three-quarters fraction (¾)

    ‰   Per mille sign (‰)

    €   Euro sign (€)

    …   Ellipsis ( )

    –   En dash (–)

    —   Em dash (—): used to indicate a sudden break in thought.

    —   Horizontal bar (―): long dash introducing quoted text.

    White space: This is not a symbol. It is nothing but empty space. But the way you exploit it does make a difference, especially with typography.

The Last Word

In its essence, typography is a powerful medium that allows for precise, effective communication. On the Web, typography can be used to enhance content, turning lifeless chunks of data into vivid, elegant conversations. But one has to thoroughly consider numerous typographic details, not only typeface and the context in which it will appear, but also measure, leading, tracking, contrast and font size. Composition aids such as grids and vertical rhythm provide a powerful framework for creating harmonious layouts in which typography can breathe and serve its purpose.

Proper paragraph formatting, judicious use of white space and typographic hierarchy and scale can improve the structure of text, making it easier to scan and read. Besides, close attention to the quality of body copy, including punctuation marks, empty spaces and special characters, contributes to a better reading experience and has a major impact on the usability of the overall design. Because Web typography is all about communication with users, you better make sure that your conversation is rich and meaningful: your readers will appreciate it. ∎

Usability principles

for
modern websites

👤 Andrew Maier   👤 David Leggett

Designing a usable website is an ambitious goal for any designer. To accomplish this, every step we take as experience designers should bring our websites closer to meeting our users' expectations. It's a slow process. We now build and test designs incrementally until we reach this unified goal. This contrasts with the way websites and Web applications have been designed in the past.

Traditionally, usability experts have interviewed users after a website was designed, built and launched to help the website's owners align their interfaces with the users' expectations. It bears repeating that after the website has launched is an extremely bad time to learn about interface errors. Fixing faulty interactions at this stage is possibly twice as expensive. Therefore it's important to get working knowledge of usability under your belt and to design in stages, testing early and testing often.

> Keep in mind that a designer's opinion is not (in most cases) your users' opinion.

We don't know a single Web designer who wouldn't want an outsider's opinion of their website. Bonus points if you find a *designer* willing to give you feedback. Keep in mind, though, that a designer's opinion isn't your *users'* opinion. To identify with our users, we must focus on much more than the outward appearance of our websites, as difficult as that is to do.

To complicate matters, modern websites quickly become huge multi-faceted structures. Competing websites often offer similar functionality, but one will win out because it provides a superior user experience. This is where the Web is headed, a sort of evolution of website design.

Creating a great user experience takes a little bit of skill, a little bit of luck and a lot of detailed work. Those details are what your users will notice again and again; and they're easy to overlook: the field of user experience encompasses many related disciplines: visual design, information architecture and usability analysis, to name a few. In this chapter, we'll touch on each of these related topics and provide examples and practical advice you can use to build a website from scratch or re-tool an existing design.

How Do Users Think?

Basically, users' habits on the Web aren't that different from customers' habits in a store. Visitors glance at each new page, scan some of the text and then click on the first link that catches their interest or vaguely resembles the thing that they're looking for. In fact, there are large parts of the page that they don't even look at.

Most users search for something interesting (or useful) and clickable; as soon as a promising candidate is found, users click. If the new page doesn't meet their expectations, the "Back" button is clicked and the search process continues.

- **Users appreciate quality and credibility.** If they see high-quality content, they are usually willing to tolerate advertisements and a poor design. This is why websites with mediocre designs but high-quality content gain a lot of traffic over the years. Content is more important than the design that supports it.

- **Users don't read; they scan.** When they analyze a Web page, users search for some fixed points or anchors that can guide them through the content on the rest of the page.

- **Web users are impatient and insist on instant gratification.** A very simple principle: if a website doesn't meet users' expectations, then the designer has failed to perform his or her job properly, and the company will lose money. The higher the cognitive load needed by users to process the website and the less intuitive the navigation, the more likely users will leave the website in search of alternatives.

- **Users don't always make the best choices.** They don't look for the quickest way to find the information they want. Nor do they scan Web pages in a linear fashion, going sequentially from one section to another. Instead, users choose whatever "satisfices" (satisfy + suffice). They choose the first reasonable option that presents itself. As soon as they find a link that might possibly lead to their goal, users will very likely click on it immediately. Optimizing is hard, and it takes a long time. Satisficing is more efficient.

- **Users follow their intuition.** In most cases, users muddle through on their own rather than read the information a designer has provided. According to Steve Krug[1], the basic reason for this is that users don't care. "If we find something that works, we stick to it. It doesn't matter to us if we understand how things work, as long as we can use them. If your audience is going to act like you're designing billboards, then design great billboards".

- **Users want to have control.** Users want to be able to control their browser and rely on consistently presented data throughout the website. For example, they don't want new windows popping up unexpectedly, and they want to be able to use the "Back" button to return to a website they had just visited.

Use a Clean and Consistent Visual Design

Visual design tells a user how to interact with the website. If the interface is well constructed, users will spend less time learning how to use the website and more time actually using it.

Unfortunately, we often let our creative side take control of the design process and, as a result, end up with an interface that is too innovative for the user to understand at first glance. There's nothing wrong with being creative, but when conventions are sacrificed for new approaches to common problems, users are forced to relearn to use things that they're already familiar with.

When approaching the visual design of a website, understanding some common conventions can go a long way towards creating a website that looks great and requires no brain power to use.

Certain elements belong in certain places

When reading a newspaper, people are accustomed to finding the paper's name at the top, a date somewhere nearby, followed quickly by headlines. Books may have some variation in their style, material and design, but a

---

1 Don't Make Me Think: A Common Sense Approach to Web Usability – New Riders

Newspapers have conventions that people intuitively understand, such as a title and date at the top, featured headlines and author names appearing beside their stories. Like newspapers, websites have their own conventions that people understand without explanation.

few things about them are always predictable, such as title, author and descriptive summary.

Similarly, people have certain expectations when they visit a website, expectations that, if not met, could result in them having trouble understanding how it works. Therefore, it's important that websites are designed so that users can *predict* how things will work and where certain elements will be.

Examples of common website conventions:

- A website's header, linked to the home page, is usually displayed in the top-left of a website. If a user wants to return to the home page, this is how they expect to do that, no matter what website they are visiting.
- **Taglines** or secondary headlines are usually located in close proximity to, and below, a website's header. The tagline quickly explains what the website is about.
- The website's search box is usually found in the top-right or top-center of a website.

- **Different** kinds of websites may have common practices of their own For example, when visiting a blog that offers subscriptions through RSS, a user will almost certainly first check the top-right of the page for subscription options.

Search is simple

Search was not always as easy as it is now. All sorts of search parameters had to be tweaked to get satisfactory results. Since then, innovators such as Amazon and Google have set a new standard for search: type something in, click a button and let the website figure out what you want. Searching is no longer an arduous process that changes from website to website. More often than not, it can be carried out using a simple input field and a button that says "Search".

There are times when straying from this basic design is reasonable, but the search function should usually at least work without the user needing additional information. For example, if adding a drop-down menu to allow users to restrict their queries brings a benefit, by all means add a drop-down menu, but the search function should still work without the drop-down menu being used.

People use this search format on Google millions of times a day. It's safe to say that users understand how this interface works without putting any thought into it.

And this is where the design of the search box becomes important. The box must be clearly visible, quickly recognizable and easy to use. One may think that the search box doesn't need a design; after all, it's just two simple elements: an input field and submit button. How much harm could a poor design do? Well, a number of things can go wrong; for instance, the text displayed in the input field may be hard to read, or the input field may be too short or too long. Some designers even prefer a minimalist solution and don't provide a submit button at all: the "Return" key has to be used instead. Well, that's not the most usable solution out there.

A search box should be a box. Your visitors don't read the page; they scan it. The most common design for the search function is a box, with the input field being a relatively wide box. Users tend to scan for this pattern on a Web page, so as good practice, try to avoid any other kind of design, such as linked text or a button without a text field.

Also, a search box should be simple. According to usability studies, it is more user-friendly to have no advanced search options displayed by default. Advanced search, as the name indicates, is advanced, and some users get confused trying to use it. One study shows that most users don't know how to use advanced search or Boolean search query syntax[2].

There are many places to put the search box, but only a couple of right ones. The most convenient spot for users would be the top center or top right of every page on your website, where users could easily find it using the common F-shaped scanning pattern. However, some blogs tend to place the search box at the bottom of the (left or right) sidebar. That's probably not a good idea but is likely done because of advertising considerations.

Links should look like links
Users should never have to guess if something is clickable or not. Traditionally, color and underlining have been used together to convey that a piece of text functions as a link. Used together, this combination continues to be the most recognizable form of linking in text.

Some things worth keeping in mind when creating links:

- Clickable items should stick out from everything else. Color alone doesn't always do a link justice, because a website usually has colored elements that aren't links. This is why the combination of color and underlining is a safe indication that something is clickable.
- Don't make non-links appear clickable by using the color and underlining combination. This can confuse the user as to what is clickable.
- Try to use the same style for all links in a certain area and from page to page. Don't use different colors for links, and don't underline some links and not others.

2 Search: Visible and Simple http://www.useit.com/alertbox/20010513.htm

- **Links** should have different states. When styling links, pay attention to their hover, active and visited states. This way, users will know when they're hovering over a link, when they've pressed it and when they've visited that page before.

Use drop-down menus only when necessary

Drop-down menus aren't bad and absolutely have their place on the Web, but they are often misused, too. In general, drop-downs are used to allow users to select an attribute from a list of possible values.

Because drop-down menus often take up so little space, they have become the preferred means of navigation for some designers. While this new direction is catching on, drop-downs have their disadvantages:

- **Links** in the drop-down menu have low visibility: unless the menu is expanded, the user will be able to see only one of their options.
- **When** a drop-down menu has too many options, the user has to scroll to see everything. Traditional lists may work better in this case.
- **Drop-downs** are not the first thing users intuitively look for as a way to navigate. Testing how effective they are on your website compared to normal navigation menus is probably best before choosing them.

However, drop-down menus do not have to be small. According to Jacob Nielsen's study on drop-down menus, so-called "mega" drop-down navigation menus work well[3]. Apparently, big two-dimensional drop-down panels that group navigation options relieve users from having to scroll and can accurately present the user's choices through effective use of typography, icons and tooltips.

Drop-down menus can organize content into small uncluttered elements but, if not done correctly, can be just as bad as a messy layout. Good practice is to avoid using drop-downs for menus that have more than two navigation levels. If the sub-menus are revealed on hover, the user will lose focus of them whenever the mouse pointer moves away from them. If the sub-menus are revealed upon being clicked, too many buttons will have to be pressed and the menu won't work nicely.

3 http://www.useit.com/alertbox/mega-dropdown-menus.html

The website shown below (Brita.de) makes this mistake. The menus are very difficult to use because if you even slightly lose focus of the menu with the mouse pointer, you have to start from the top. Notice the tooltip, which also gets in the way of the navigation. In fact, it is a good idea to remove tooltips from drop-down navigation altogether to make sub-menu items scannable and readable.

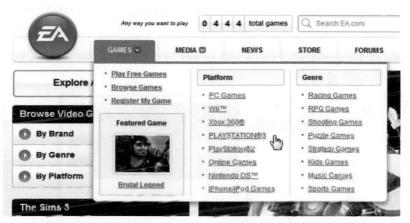

A nice, clean and well-organized mega drop-down menu on EA.com. Notice the visual indicators next to the "Games" and "Media" list items, making it clear to visitors that further navigation options are available in the drop-down menus.

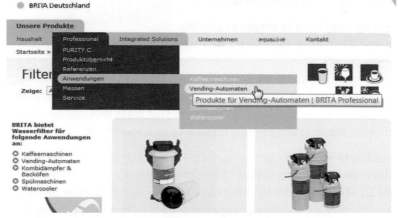

The drop-down menu on Brita.de is hardly usable. It contains multiple levels of navigation, requires horizontal scrolling and displays tooltips that make it impossible to scan the other navigation options. Not very user-friendly.

Avoiding many drop-down levels may be too much of a restriction for the type of navigation you are trying to create. One solution, though, might improve the usability of the hover function and multi-level navigation. With most menus, the drop-down list disappears immediately once the user moves the mouse pointer away from the menu. The solution is to delay its disappearance. Or, add a click function that requires users to click outside the drop-down menu area to close it, similar to how a Lightbox functions.

Consider the menu on Porsche's website below. It has multiple levels, but the menu has a wide focus range, so you have to move your pointer a certain distance away from the menu to close it. It is a good design solution.

Porsche has a large mega drop-down menu. The navigation is user-friendly because the menus have a wide focus range.

Make sign-up forms as simple as possible

Designing effective Web forms isn't easy, and for one simple reason: nobody likes to fill in forms, neither offline nor online. Unless your product or service is some revolutionary ideas that will impress visitors at first glance, throwing up any sign-up form onto your website is simply not enough. Coming to sound design decisions that make completion of the form easy, intuitive and painless for your users is important.

According to the results of our "Sign-Up Form Design Survey[4]", the registration link is most often titled "Sign up" (40%) and placed in the upper-right corner. Sign-up forms often have a simple layout to avoid distracting users; they are usually one page and attract visitors by explaining the benefits of registration.

4 http://www.smashingmagazine.com/2008/07/04/web-form-design-patterns-sign-up-forms/

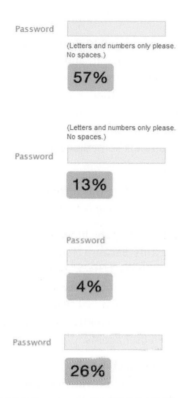

Hints often appear below the input field (57%) or to the right of the field (26%).

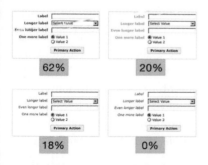

Titles of input fields are highlighted bold (62%), and input field labels are usually right-aligned.

Titles of input fields are highlighted bold (62%), and input field labels (when placed on the left hand side of the input fields) are usually right-aligned. The form's design is usually kept as simple as possible: designers tend to use few mandatory fields (three to five) and few optional fields (two or fewer). Vertically arranged fields are clearly preferred to horizontally arranged fields. No predominant trends in the alignment of labels (i.e. to the right, to the left or above input fields) could be identified.

Sign-up forms usually do not contain any distractions and let the user focus on task at hand. They usually have no hover, active or focus effects. Hints often appear below the input field (57%) or to the right of the field (26%).

Email confirmation is usually not used (82%), but password confirmation is common (72%). Also notable, the "Cancel" button is almost never used, the "Submit" button is left-aligned (56%) or centered (26%), while Captchas are used on every other form. Lastly, thank-you messages are often used to motivate users to continue exploring the services of the website.

Consider adding "back to top" links

Unfortunately, this friendly service – letting users jump to the top of the page – is offered rarely. Most designers don't include it, and there is a reason for that: "back to top" links are not always useful. For example, they may be unnecessary for websites that have rather short pages or articles. Clicking on a "top" link on a page whose entire content is visible would produce no effect and would be rather irritating. The variety of screen resolutions these days makes the "top" link sometimes unusable and unnecessary.

However, websites with long pages can offer visitors this nifty feature, which saves time and avoids the need for vertical scrolling with the mouse.

One major problem with "top" links is that they affect the browser's navigation buttons and "pollute" the browsing history. Because "top" links are anchors like any other links, clicking on the browser's "Back" button will take users to the foot of the page that they are currently viewing, not to the previous page. In addition, accessibility experts claim that "Back to top" links are vague in concept, are not implemented consistently across websites and may disrupt the use of speech-based user agents.

"Back to top" links are often used in FAQs, help sections and site maps, where they help divide chapters or paragraphs and provide users with a quick way to jump to the beginning of the page, where the main navigation appears.

Avoid splash pages if possible

A splash screen is the front page of a website that doesn't provide any actual content but rather offers visitors some kind of intimation of, or background information about, the website. Designers use splash pages in their portfolios as eye candy to impress potential clients. Companies tend to make use of them to draw the attention of visitors to their latest products. And users can't stand them because they usually take a long time to load and provide almost no navigation options, except to "Enter the site".

Depending on the designer's creativity, splash pages can have attractive visual elements. Some have interactive Flash movies that start playing automatically (a usability nightmare for users with multiple tabs opened). They usually have a very simple structure, mostly just an image with few lines of text and links. A splash page doesn't always follow the design of the rest of the website.

Although most websites don't have them, splash pages remain popular because they are sometimes necessary, for instance, to display disclaimers, important messages (approaching deadline, critical updates, etc.), website requirements (Flash, Java, QuickTime, etc.) or hints for browsing (typical on Flash websites). Splash pages are also used to let users select their preferred viewing mode (standard or full-screen), speed (low or high bandwidth) and language (although language options can and should be integrated in the main layout). Bottom line: users don't like splash pages, and "creative" splash pages get on their nerves.

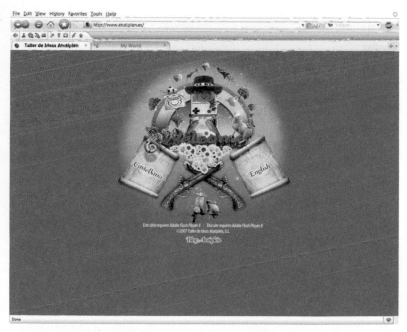

A typical splash page, with a welcome message and language selection links.

Links should open in the same window

Initially, the decision of whether to open links in a new window might seem to depend on the individual website and the preference of visitors. Visitors to websites with a lot of external links may be more tolerant of links opening in a new window, not wanting to have to do it manually. Visitors to websites with less external links may want to be able to pick which pages to open in a new window to browse through afterward. However, this is not always true.

From a usability standpoint, forcing links to open in a new window violates one of the fundamental principles of user interface design: users should always be in control of the interface. Users want consistency in their interfaces and need to know that their interactions won't be disrupted. Any deviation from this principle makes the website more design-oriented and less user-oriented . As Shneiderman notes, experienced us-

Users should always be able to choose whether a link opens in the current tab or in a new tab or window.

ers have a strong desire to know that they are in charge of the system and that the system will respond to their actions.

The main problem with forcing links to open in a new window is that the decision overrides the user's decision to control the behavior of their browser. Let's consider two situations in which a user doesn't know up front if a website will open links in a new window or in the same window:

1. The user wants to open links in a new window, but the website opens them in the same window.
2. The user wants to open links in the same window, but the website opens them in a new window.

In the first situation, the user can choose to open a link in a new window using the context menu or a shortcut. Here, the user is the initiator of action because she or he decides how the linked page will be displayed. The website's behavior meets the user's expectations, resulting in a good experience.

In the second situation, the user clicks on a link only to find that it suddenly opens in a new window. Here, the user is the recipient of action and has to respond to how the new page opens (which could very well by closing it right away). The website's behavior doesn't meet the user's expectations, resulting in a bad experience.

Users are annoyed when a website does something that they have not told it to do. If opening a page in a new window would be more convenient, let users do it themselves; don't insult their intelligence by making decisions for them. Don't force new windows upon users unless you have a very good reason to do it.

Usability checkpoints that you should be aware of

1. **Don't change the user's window size.** This argument is similar to the one against pop-ups. Some browsers, such as Internet Explorer, save their dimensions for further sessions. As Ben Bodien states, "It's just plain inconsiderate to assume that you know better than the user how their software environment should be configured".

2. **Don't make font sizes too small.** Long passages are harder to read in a small font size. Don't make links, buttons, forms, search boxes or other elements too small either. Also, make sure any content blocks have between 50 and 85 characters per line, and provide sufficient white space around your text.

3. **Write clear link text.** Links should describe the destination they lead to. Avoid ambiguous descriptions.

4. **Remove dead links.** Too many of them are out there. Why would you point visitors to a dead end?

5. **Proofread.** Read everything. Even if you've already read it, read it again. Get someone else to read it, too. You'll always pick up on something that has to change. See if you can reduce the text by keeping it specific. Break up large blocks into shorter paragraphs. Add clear headings throughout, and use lists so that users can scan easily.

   Don't forget about dynamic text, too, such as alert boxes. Check that important terms aren't widowed or orphaned in your paragraphs and that punctuation marks are used correctly, particularly apostrophes, quotation marks, hyphens and dashes.

6. **Check functionality.** Test everything thoroughly. If you have a contact form, test it to see what comes through. Get others to test your website, and not just family and friends but the website's target audience. Sit back and watch how they use the website. It's amazing what you'll pick up on when others use your website differently than how you assume they'd use it. Common things to check for are contact forms, search functions, shopping baskets and log-in areas.

7. **Keep the Web form as simple as possible.** Use the right form elements for the right tasks (radio buttons, check boxes, input areas, text areas), provide enough space (with enough padding) for comfortable typing, remove unnecessary fields and provide descriptive labels for each input field (adding help information and hints as needed). Also, do not force users to use restrictive input formats (for example, the system

should be able to understand when users type their phone number with or without brackets, hyphens and spaces). Also, provide informative and helpful error messages.

8. **Degrade gracefully.** Your website should work with JavaScript turned off. Users often have JavaScript turned off for security reasons, so be prepared for this. Test your forms to make sure they still perform server-side validation checks, and test any cool AJAX stuff you have going on.

9. **Don't forget about defensive design.** The most commonly overlooked defensive design element is the 404 page. If a user requests a page that doesn't exist, your 404 page will be displayed. Get your users back on track by providing a useful 404 page that directs them to the home page or suggests other pages they may be interested in. Also check your forms for validation. Try submitting unusual information in the form fields (a lot of characters, letters in number fields, etc.), and make sure if any errors occur, the user is provided with enough feedback to be able to fix it.

10. **Don't forget about the print style sheet.** If users want to print a page from your website, chances are they want only the main content and not the navigation or extra design elements. That's why creating a print-specific style sheet is a good idea. Also, certain CSS elements, such as floated text blocks, do not always come out well when printed.

11. **Strive for optimal performance.** You'll want to configure your website for optimal performance. You should do this on an ongoing basis after launch, but you can take a few simple steps before launch, too. Reducing HTTP requests, using CSS sprites wherever possible, optimizing images for the Web, compressing JavaScript and CSS files and so on can all help load your pages more quickly and use less server resources.

12. **Make it easy to contact you.** Perhaps you just don't want to be contacted, but if visitors want to get in touch with you and can't find any contact information, you will lose their interest and trust. This is disastrous for online stores and a missed opportunity for every website.

Convey Your Website's Organization

In *The Elements of User Experience*, Jesse James Garrett introduces the concept of the website skeleton. In simple terms, the skeleton helps determine what form a website's functionality will take. Here is some context: Garrett's posits that the realm of user experience on the Web can be approached from two different perspectives: either as a software interface (as in the case of Web applications) or as a hypertext system (which would be the "content" part of content management systems).

A website, though, is rarely defined entirely by its content or entirely by its functionality. Whatever the case, we must always convey organization.

Girlgamer.com uses color themes to differentiate sections of its website. The differences are relatively subtle but allow sections of the website to stand on their own.

Designing interfaces that are easy to use and unambiguous is the realm of *interface design*. If our website is more content-driven, then we have to help users get to this content. This is known as *navigation design*. In both cases, we want to help users make sense of the information available to them on our website, using information design. To reiterate: interface design helps users do things, navigation design helps users go places and information design helps our website communicate. All of these areas should be addressed before considering a website's visual design.

Use signposts to build context

Employing distinct colors, headers and buttons for each section of your website can help orient visitors. These are known as signposts. Website signposts function like the "You are here" label on information kiosks at malls and amusement parks. This is why making links open in a new window degrades the user experience: the visitor loses context. Users who know where they are on your website have a better chance of developing a sense of purpose and asking themselves "What can I do here?" This is the goal of information design; empowering users to make choices with the information available to them.

Consider a business such as a daycare, whose website must appeal to a diverse audience. One section of the website could use atypical typography, whimsical copy, cartoon characters and bright colors to appeal to children, while another section of the website could use a refined typeface, direct copy, abstract images and a muted color scheme to appeal to adults. This way the website appeals to a wide audience but targets unique messages to distinct segments using signposts.

Establish good navigation

Navigation is arguably the most important part of your website, aside from the content. Luckily for us, we can capitalize on a number of conventions to connect our design decisions to our navigation. In most cases, users simply try to answer the question "Where can I go?" But the answer isn't always as straightforward as they would like. In general, users of any content-heavy website expect up to three types of navigation on any given page.

Global navigation: Where can I go in the overall website?

Global navigation generally comes in the form of tabular navigation, in addition to containing a convenient link to the website's home page. Global navigation should contain "controlled" words and phrases (such as common section names, industry-standard terms or layman's terms) and reinforce the website's structure. Because global navigation, if well positioned, will be the first place users go, its design is extremely important.

Local navigation: Where can I go within this section?

Many users like to explore content related to what they are viewing, and local navigation fits the bill. If your website is well organized, users will know what they will find when they arrive at a section, and local navigation is their gateway to this content.

Because local navigation is a common reason for users to stay on a website, many websites now have a sort of hybrid navigation. For example, after performing a search on Amazon, users can jump right into browsing by that category using the local navigation, which appears precisely where they would expect it to appear.

Contextual navigation: Where can I go on this page?

Contextual navigation is an under-used but valuable form of navigation. After users descend into the depths of your website and have found the content they were searching for, where else can they go? Contextual navigation keeps users on the same page but allows them to move around using digestible chunks.

> Contextual navigation is an under-used but valuable form of navigation.

When creating contextual navigation, put the menu (which is usually a table of contents or list of article's categories) at the top of the content and include "Back to top" links throughout the page's sections. When executed correctly, contextual navigation turns pages on your website into resources, encouraging users to come back often for its information. Think about how useful any page on Wikipedia can be. More importantly, contextual navigation provides a unique (and often overlooked) opportunity to cross-sell, promote and inform the user while helping to build the website's brand.

Supplemental navigation

After exploring a page of your website, many users will jump ship and visit another website or close their browser. A good idea, then, is to put supplemental navigation immediately after your content. Supplemental navigation frequently includes related content and invites your readers to stick around and learn what else your website offers.

A "breadcrumb" (or "breadcrumb trail") is a type of secondary navigation scheme that discloses the user's location in a website or Web application. The term comes from the Hansel and Gretel fairy tale in which the two title children drop breadcrumbs to form a trail back to their home. Just like in the tale, breadcrumbs in real-world applications offer users a way to trace the path back to their original landing point.

Now What?

You've reached the end of this post. Seeing you made it this far means you might be interested in these related articles and resources:

9 Design Blogs to Follow in 2009

Tutorial9 Presents: The Gift of Knowledge

Our Favorite Tutorial Indexes, Directories and Feeds

The New Tutorial9

After reading an article on tutorial9.net, readers are presented with a list of related articles on the website. This is an example of contextual navigation.

You can usually find breadcrumbs in websites that have a lot of content organized hierarchically. You also see them in Web applications that have more than one step, where they function like a progress bar. In their simplest form, breadcrumbs are horizontally arranged text links separated by the "greater than" symbol (>); the symbol indicates the level of that page relative to the page links beside it.

Consequently, it is a good idea to use breadcrumb navigation if your site is large and has hierarchically arranged pages. E-commerce websites are a perfect example: a large variety of products grouped into logical categories. You shouldn't use breadcrumbs for single-level websites that have no logical hierarchy or grouping. A great way to determine if a website would benefit from breadcrumb navigation is to construct a site map or diagram representing the website's navigation architecture, and then analyze whether breadcrumbs would improve the user's ability to navigate within and between categories.

Breadcrumb navigation should be regarded as an extra feature and shouldn't replace primary navigation menus. It's a convenience, a secondary scheme that reminds users where they are and gives them an alternative way to navigate your website.

Breadcrumbs in Apple's store appear underneath the main navigation. This is an example of the supplemental navigation.

By offering a breadcrumb trail for all pages on a large multi-level website, you enable users to return to higher-level categories in fewer clicks than they would need using the browser's "Back" button or the primary navigation. And because they are usually laid out horizontally and plainly styled, breadcrumb trails don't take up a lot of space on the page.

Breadcrumb trails can be a great way to entice first-time visitors to peruse a website upon viewing the landing page. If users arrive on a particular page through a Google search, seeing a breadcrumb trail may tempt them to click to higher-level pages to view related topics of interests. This, in turn, reduces the overall bounce rate of the website.

Important Usability Rules and Principles

7±2 Principle

Because the human brain is limited in its capacity to process information, it deals with complexity by dividing information into chunks and units. According to George A. Miller's studies, humans can retain only about five to nine things in their short-term memory at one time. This is often used as an argument for limiting the number of items in a navigation menu to seven. But the debate about the "Seven, Plus or Minus Two[5]" myth is heated. So it's not clear how the 7±2 principle can or should be applied to the Web.

2-Second Rule

This is a loose principle that a user shouldn't have to wait more than two seconds for certain types of system responses, such as application switching and application launching. The choice of two seconds is somewhat arbitrary but a reasonable order of magnitude. A more reliable principle is, the less users have to wait, the better will be their experience.

3-Click Rule

According to this rule, users stop using a website if they aren't able to find the information they are looking for or access the website's feature within three mouse clicks. The rule highlights the importance of clear navigation, a logical structure and an easy-to-follow website hierarchy. In most situa-

5   http://www.ddj.com/184412300

tions, the number of clicks is irrelevant, though; what is important is that visitors always know where they are, where they were and where they can go next. Even ten clicks is okay if users still feel they have a complete understanding of how the system works.

80/20 Rule (Pareto Principle)

The Pareto principle (also known as the Law of the Vital Few and the principle of factor sparsity) states that 80% of the effects come from 20% of the causes. This is a basic rule of thumb in business ("80% of your sales come from 20% of your clients") but can also be applied to design and usability. For instance, dramatic improvements can be achieved by identifying the 20% of users, customers, activities, products or processes that account for 80% of your profit and then maximizing the attention you pay to them.

Eight Golden Rules of Interface Design

From his interface design studies, Ben Shneiderman has proposed a collection of principles that were derived heuristically from experience and that apply to most interactive systems. These principles are relevant to all user interfaces and, as such, also apply to Web design.

1. Strive for consistency.
2. Allow frequent users to use shortcuts.
3. Offer informative feedback.
4. Design dialogs to yield closure.
5. Offer simple error handling.
6. Permit easy reversal of actions.
7. Impart a sense of control. Support an internal locus of control.
8. Reduce short-term memory load.

Fitts' Law

Identified by Paul Fitts in 1954, Fitts' Law is a model of human movement that predicts the time required to rapidly move to a target area, as a function of the distance to the target and the size of the target. The law claims that there is a speed-accuracy trade off associated with pointing, whereby targets that are smaller and/or further away require more time to acquire. The law is usually invoked when dealing with the mouse movements that visitors have to make to get from point A to point B. The principle encourages content to be positioned in areas that maximize their accessibility and improve click rates.

Inverted Pyramid

The inverted pyramid is a writing style that puts a summary at the very top of the article. It is essentially a "waterfall effect", well-known in journalism, whereby writers give their readers an instant picture of the topic they're reporting about. The article begins with the conclusion, followed by key points and then minor details, such as background information. Because Web users want instant gratification, the inverted pyramid style[6] significantly improves the user experience.

Give Users a 50,000-Foot View of Your Application

When exploring your website for the first time, some users may feel overwhelmed. Getting a holistic understanding of what your website is trying to convey can be difficult unless you present your information effectively. A number of ways to organize content exist, and we should consider them all carefully. Before we do that, let's consider some careers related to this task.

Professional architects create structures that perform a specific function. If an architect is commissioned to build an auditorium, she may begin by researching acoustics. How should the performance hall be designed to optimize the listening experience? The architect is hired to give the intended function a defined form.

Now, consider the librarian's task: to organize a huge body of information. A library is simply somewhere where books are stored. But imagine trying to find a particular book in an disorganized library. A library without an organization scheme would be hard pressed to keep its doors open.

Now, let's return to websites. Organizing any website that has a lot of content or that needs maximum functionality requires knowledge of both of these disciplines, but adapted to websites: we call this information architecture. Information architecture is the organization of a website's content

6 http://www.useit.com/alertbox/9606.html

in a way that best communicates what the website offers visitors. Let's look at some ways you can convey your website's goals.

Mental models and metaphor

Likewise, users go to your website to get things done. They appreciate the visual design and clever imagery, but after their initial visit, they simply want to use your website as part of their normal routine.

Therefore, consider using metaphors to present your service. Metaphors are a wonderfully easy way to communicate your product or service and require little explanation, because good ones closely align your product or service with information (or mental models) already inside your users' heads.

Organize your website's content

People have a mental "road map" of how things function in their day-to-day lives. For example, on any given morning, a person knows that they have to wake to the alarm clock, eat some cereal, read the news, shower, dress and then drive to work. All of these processes are a part of their morning routine and are how they get things done.

Amazon calls the repository of items you intend to purchase your "shopping cart", when in fact it's just a list of items in the company's database. Why does Amazon do this? Because a shopping cart is a convenient metaphor for the complicated technical things that go on to make your list of items persist as you continue browsing the website. Of course, if you're shopping on Amazon.co.uk, it is referred to as a "shopping basket.

If your website contains a significant amount of content, you will need to find a sensible way to organize it. A good place to start is with categorization, separating your content into semantically coherent groups. The ideal solution requires the least amount of overhead and is most useful to your users. To create a sensible categorization schema, develop a taxonomy based words and phrases that your audience would expect.

Another way to organize your content (and improve your website's search results) is to make use of meta data, or data about your data. Meta data sounds complicated until you realize you've dealt with it for quite a while. For example, meta data about a blog article includes things like author, date of publication, view count and number of comments. This kind of data allows users to search and sort your website's content, which in turn gives them actionable lists of content, driving them closer to their goals.

Ikea makes great use of navigation. Across the top, IKEA aficionados can quickly get to the latest and greatest furniture by clicking "New." And if you're looking for a particular item, IKEA offers a well-organized site map.

Offer a site map

If your website contains a lot of content, a site map is a good way to orient users. A site map is a page or section that displays a reasonably comprehensive subset of the pages available on your website. Consider displaying this structure in your footer or making its availability known by providing links to it.

Getting Started guides

Offering a "Getting Started" guide is one of the most straightforward ways to inform users about your website. Unfortunately, it is also one of the bits of content on your website that is least likely to be read. Most users simply ignore large blocks of text that describe how a service works. It's just not how people use the Web.

As such, a number of best practices have emerged to aid in helping to show users how a website works, practices that don't rely on large blocks of text. Here are a couple of ways to offer a getting-started guide with little to no text.

Blank Slates

Blank slates provide a visual way to orient your users. The idea is simple: show an image of how your website would look with data in it. By seeing an example of how a website or application looks with data, users get an idea of how to interact with it.

Product Tours and Inline Help

Consider documenting your product throughout the interface. The current fashion for large multi-columned layouts makes it easier than ever to embed this kind of documentation on a website. If a user has a question about a particular feature, they can see the answer without ever leaving the page.

Build Trust

Trust is easily one of the most important things your website must establish with its users. Trust is a simple principle that's difficult to articulate yet extremely important. Much research aligns positive user experiences with a feeling of trust in the website itself.

Work to build trust: think of all of the things in your life that you trust, and then ask yourself, "Why do I trust them"? Think of credibility, transparency and generosity; respect your users and show your appreciation of their trust and engagement.

Motigo allows users to quickly and easily see how their dashboard would look once they've added content.

Don't allow users to ruin their own experience

Fortunately, this advice is usually followed on modern websites. While it applies mainly to Web applications, it is also good food for thought for content-driven websites. Always expect users to test your application's limits. If users can delete content, give them an "Undo" function.

If users can close the browser while writing a message, don't throw away their data without asking. If users can close the browser in the middle of saving a document, don't delete the data. In all cases, anticipate that the user will deviate from the way that you intend for them to use your service, and don't make the consequences undesirable.

Don't require too much and deliver too little

In their effort to design the latest and greatest interaction, many designers lose sight of one of their principal charges as experience designers:

don't break anything. Some designers know better than that, but modern Web designs certainly aren't without their hiccups. So let it be made clear: any functionality that is a part of the user's browser shouldn't be divorced from the user's experience of your website.

The most fundamental elements often break first. Don't kill the user's "Back" button. Don't restrict the user's ability to bookmark pages of your website. And don't unnecessarily modify the user's visited and unvisited link colors. Many beginner and intermediate users rely heavily on these features to navigate the Web. The functionality of their browser is essential to their experience.

5	TOP	Everything Is Illuminated	★★★★☆	Drama	Now	×
		Robin Hood: Men in Tights has been removed				Undo
7	TOP	Secretary	★★★★☆	Independent	Now	×
8	TOP	Sixteen Candles	★★★★☆	Romance	Now	×

When an item from your Netflix queue is deleted, the service gives you the option to undo your action.

On a larger scale, a more pervasive distrust is brooding between interactive designers and their users. Many interactions should be cross-browser tested and must gracefully degrade in the absence of browser features that users can disable. It should go without saying, but a usable Web is, by definition, an accessible Web.

Finally, let users know if they are using a browser that your website does not support. Don't leave them guessing. Only when you tell them will they know they can enlist to fight in the browser war.

Test Early, Test Often

The so-called TETO principle should be applied to every Web design project because usability tests often provide crucial insights into significant problems and issues with layout.

Test not too late, not too little and not for the wrong reasons. As for testing for the right reasons, understanding that most design decisions are local is important; you can't categorically answer whether one layout is better than another because you need to analyze each one from a very specific point of view (taking into account requirements, stakeholders, budget, etc.).

MailChimp shows a demo video on its home page to ensure that users get started quickly.

Some important points to keep in mind:

- **According** to Steve Krug, testing one user is 100% better than testing none, and testing one user early in the project is better than testing fifty near the end. According to Boehm's First Law, errors are most frequent during the requirements and design stages and become more expensive the later they are removed.

- **Testing** is an iterative process, meaning that you design something, test it, fix it and then test it again. You may find problems that were overlooked during the first round because users were preoccupied with other problems.

- **Usability** tests always produce useful results. They point either to problems with functionality and interactivity or to major design flaws, which in both cases are useful insights for your project.

- According to Weinberg's Law, a developer is unsuited to test his or her own code. This holds true for designers as well. After you've worked on a website for a few weeks, you can't see it with fresh eyes anymore. You know how it was built and therefore know exactly how it works; you have the background knowledge that independent testers and visitors of your website wouldn't have.

Bottom line: if you want a great website, you've got to test.

Final Thoughts

The biggest challenge we face when we set out to improve the user experience is which consideration to tackle first! It can be frustrating but also a good position to be in. There are just so many angles you can take to make your website more enjoyable.

Make the effort, and you'll end up with a product that your users will love almost as much as you do. We hope the majority of the points discussed here apply to your project. To summarize:

- **While** creativity is good, letting our creative side take over the design process is not. Do not design an interface that is so innovative and different that an ordinary Web user wouldn't easily recognize how to use it.

- **Build** predictable websites. Design what the user expects. Do not try to build the next big Web feature unless it's absolutely a better (and more intuitive) way to complete an old task.

- **Users** browse the Web quickly. They don't stop to look at the tiny details that we as designers spend hours laboring over. They'll appreciate your work much more if you make it easy to get from one place to another and help them identify what they need. Remember, many users simply want to use your website as part of their normal routine.

- **Before** focusing on visual design, spend some time planning how your users will do things on your website (interface design), how they will navigate the website (navigation design), and how the website will communicate with them (information design).

- **Always** tell users where they are on your website using signposts. Users who can tell where they are on a website have a better chance of developing a sense of purpose.

- **Make** use of the conventions of navigation. A user who doesn't understand where they can go will have a very difficult time navigating your website. When planning the navigation, don't stop at the first level: work on the global, local and contextual navigation of every page.

- **Just** as navigation requires planning, content organization shouldn't be overlooked either. Help users find what they are looking for by keeping content organized in semantically coherent groups.

- **Always** anticipate that a user may not use your website the way you intend. Predict how they might misuse the website, and don't let the consequences of misuse be undesirable (for example, deleting a document without showing an "Undo" option). ■

The ultimate guide
to fantastic color usage
in web design, usability and experience

Darius A Monsef IV

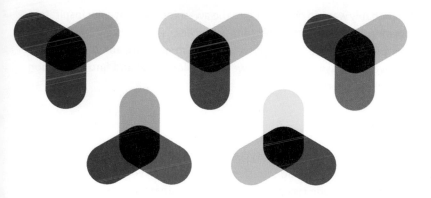

H ow can color in Web design focus attention, inform decisions, inspire action, organize information, highlight elements, balance composition and enrich experiences? We'll explore answers to these questions in this chapter and look at several examples of good color usage in websites.

Primal Needs

Researchers theorize that the color vision of primates evolved to its advanced color-sensitive state because of early needs to distinguish between different types of food, find mates and survive dangerous predators and situations[1]. Choosing between the fatally poisonous *green lantana* camara berry and the not so fatal red one would have been fairly difficult without color vision.

We are now gathering, experiencing, analyzing and sifting through information at a much faster pace than our evolutionary ancestors did, especially when it comes to websites and other media. Poor color decisions in design probably won't kill anyone, but they can produce an undesirable experience. Therefore, understanding how color can shape and enrich a visitor's experience and interaction with a design is important.

Building On The Basics

You probably want to dive right into the awesome world of color inspiration and information, but it is important to first discuss some basics about color, color theory and the language we use to communicate about color. Once we have that basic foundation, we can explore color and find inspiration everywhere in our world.

Color Primer

Our eyes have three different types of color receptors, which each respond to the red, green and blue colors of light differently. For instance, the color blue stimulates one receptor more than the others and as a result trans-

---

1   Regan, B. C., Julliot, C., Simmen, B., Vienot, F., Charles-Dominique, P. & Mollon, J. D. 2001 Fruits, foliage and the evolution of primate colour vision. Phil.Trans. R. Soc. Lond. B. 36, 229-283.

mits different information to the brain. The way in which different combinations of color affect these different receptors results in the millions of different kinds of color, called hues. These hues can be mapped to a circle (often called a color wheel) in degrees (°), with each 60° marking a different base color. Three of these base colors are called primary (red, green, blue), three are called secondary (yellow, cyan, magenta) and the six in between them are called tertiary.

A popular color model in computing is called HSB. It uses hue and two related terms, saturation and brightness, to define and describe colors. Saturation (0 to 100%) refers to how vibrant a color is compared to its maximum potential. Brightness refers to a color's lightness (0 to 100%). Pure colors have high brightness and saturation values, making them more vivid. Dark colors have low brightness values, making them blacker. The less saturated a color, the more colorless it appears, until it has no color. As you can see from the screenshot, many colors can be made just from mixing one hue degree with various shades of white, black and gray. Another screenshot demonstrates this for red at 360°.

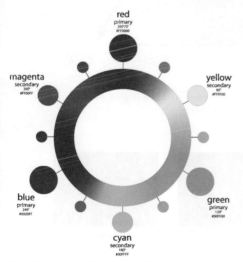

The primary colors in computer design are red, green and blue. The secondary colors, cyan, magenta and yellow, together with the primary colors make up the six distinct color hues of the color wheel. Hue values are presented in degrees (°), while hexadecimal values are labeled with the standard pound sign sign (#).

In discussing color, other terms that describe differences in colors include tint, shade and tone. Tint is the amount of white that a pure color has. Shade is the amount of black it has. Tone is the amount of gray it has. The screenshot demonstrates how a color changes based on these properties.

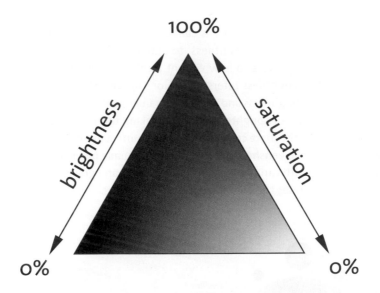

By adjusting the brightness and saturation components of a single color hue, roughly 46,000 distinct colors can be created per color hue.

It may be helpful to discuss color with reference to tint, shade and tone. When a fellow designer says, "I like the color of the logo, but it should be a darker shade", you'll know exactly what he means. Brightness and saturation are more complicated concepts and tend to mean different things to different people, making them less useful when discussing ideas about color.

Combining hue, saturation and brightness, we can create any color visible to the human eye[2]. Most computer monitors display color through a mixture of the primary red, green and blue colors. Historically, artists have used red, yellow and blue as primary colors. The print industry uses cyan, magenta, yellow and black to produce different colors. Computers use red, green and blue because monitors emit these colors of light. With a value between 0 and 255 assigned to each color, a computer monitor can produce up to 16,777,216 different colors. Red, green and blue lights mixed together at full value (R:255, G:255, B:255) produce pure white light, while the absence of these three colors (R:0, G:0, B:0) produces no light, or black. This type of color mixing is typically referred to as the RGB color model.

Colors on the Web are understood by the browser as hexadecimal values and are typically labeled with the pound sign (#). Each red, green and blue element of a color is converted from a number (0 to 255) to a set of characters that the computer can understand. At each end of this scale, 0 is represented in hexadecimal format as "00," while 255 is represented by "FF." The primary colors in their hexadecimal equivalents are #FF0000 (red), #00FF00 (green) and #0000FF (blue). Many graphics applications automatically convert HSB, RGB and hexadecimal values to each other, but a strong understanding of each will only make your life easier as a designer.

Color Theory

Color theory is the study of how pure colors relate to each other and the effect of their combinations. We'll go over some of the most recognized color relationships, or schemes, along with examples of their use on various websites today. Developing a color scheme is often the first step in deciding which colors will look best together in a design. In each of the following screenshots, the color palette shows the main colors being used in the accompanying screenshot, while the pure color hues are marked on the color wheel to show the relationships between the colors.

2   Backhaus, W., Reinhold, K. & Werner, J. S. 1998 Color Vision, Walter de Gruyter & Co.,
    New York, p. 321.

Monochromatic: one hue, varying in saturation and brightness.

Monochromatic palette.

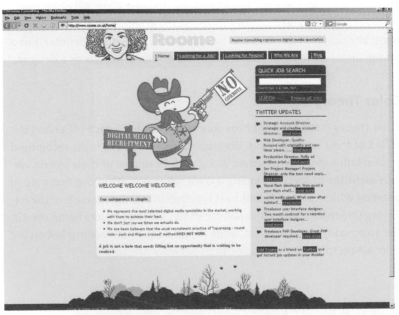

Monochromatic color scheme.

Analogous or Blend: hues adjacent to each other on the color wheel.

Analogous palette.

Analogous color scheme.

Complementary: two hues directly opposite each other on the color wheel.

Complementary palette.

Complementary color scheme.

Split-Complementary: one hue on one side of the color wheel, and the two hues adjacent to its complement.

Split-complementary palette

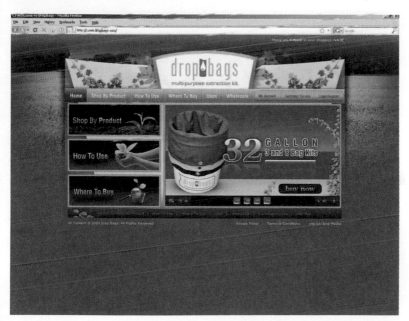

Split-complementary color scheme.

Triadic: three hues equidistant from each other on the color wheel.

Split-complementary palette.

Triadic color scheme.

Double-Complementary or Rectangular-Tetradic: two hues and their complements.

Double-Complementary palette.

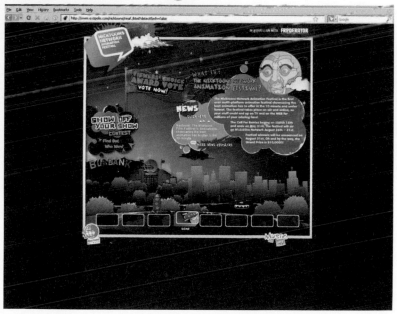

Double-Complementary color scheme.

Square-Tetradic: four hues equidistant from each other on the color wheel.

Square-Tetradic palette.

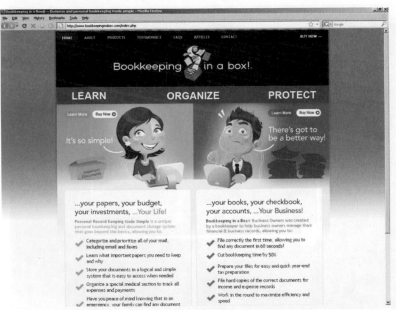

Square-Tetradic color scheme.

Analogous-Complementary: two complementary hues, and an adjacent hue of one of their complements.

Analogous Complemantary palette.

Analogous Complemantary color scheme.

Neutral: muted colors.

Neutral palette.

Neutral color scheme.

Accented: muted colors, with one color high in saturation.

Accent palette.

Accent color scheme.

Warm: colors from the top of the color wheel, with hues ranging from 271° to 90°.

Warm palette.

Warm color scheme.

Cold: colors from the bottom of the color wheel, with hues ranging from 91° to 270°.

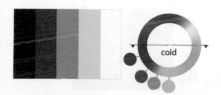

Cold palette.

CoLd color scheme.

Color And Usability

In addition to making a website look good, color can also help your audience use the website. Imagine if websites didn't evolve beyond the black text on white background aesthetic of early newspapers. In 1982, USA Today broke into the business with the first color newspaper[3]. In addition to

USA Today uses color to help readers quickly identify each section of the paper, and it has been doing this since it opened its doors in 1982.

having color pictures on many of its pages, it used color to mark each section so that readers could quickly find the sections they were interested in. This concept is important in Web design for both new and returning visitors. USA Today carried this concept through to its website by adding colored buttons that correspond to the sections in the printed version. It has chosen distinct hues for each section. Unfortunately, though, very similar blues are used for the "Home", "News" and "Travel" buttons, which probably trips up users on occasion.

3 Garcia, M. R. Jun 18 2008 The color evolution of USA Today: a three-minute interview with Richard Curtis, http://garciamedia.com/blog/articles/the_color_evolution_of_usa_today_a_three_minute_interview_with_richard_curt

Mint.com successfully uses color to help potential customers understand its service and persuade them to take action. The two most striking color elements on Mint's home page are the pleasing double-complementary palette in the personal finance data graph and the bright-orange button that says "Free! Get started here," which stands out against the light-green-tinted background.

This site also uses color to give users immediate feedback as soon as an error has occurred on its website form. Its creators chose a color that is

Double-complementary palette

Mint.com uses a double-complementary color scheme to illustrate the effectiveness of its software. The bright-orange button pops out from the screen and attracts the user's eye.

often used to alert people to danger, red, whose hue contrasts well with the pale-green base of the website, making it difficult to miss.

Color And Engagement

Color can focus a user's attention and coax them into engaging with a website. With all of the noise and attention demanded from your audience every minute of the day, it's absurd to expect them to make a concerted

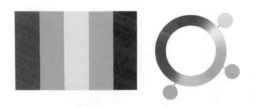

The yellow-orange and blue hues are nearly complementary colors. Highlighting the sticker in green disrupts these complements and attracts attention.

The bright-green sticker, among the slightly muted darker colors, grabs your attention.

effort to engage with your design. Your colors should pull them into the design and content. You can use color to draw their attention to the most important aspects of your website. Using very few colors, UI Tuneup explains its service quickly and then points you in the right direction to get you started using its service.

Even when your website has a lot of colors, you can draw users to a certain element by giving that element a color unique to the page. OtherInbox uses green to highlight the focal point of its website, the "Test drive" button.

One of the worst things that can happen is that a new visitor cannot figure out how to navigate your website, gets frustrated and leaves. Color can help them start on the right foot, as you'll see by comparing two websites that essentially have the same complementary color scheme and similar designs, but use them to completely different effect.

By choosing bright complementary colors, UI Tuneup makes it easy for users to find out what the service is about and where to go to begin using it.

Sonze made some of its buttons light blue and some of them deep red. But the blue is so light that the user has to struggle to read what the button says, if they even find it. Also, clickable items have little consistency in color, and so even if you find the said buttons, you may not find the other clickable items.

These two websites have similar colors schemes, but each achieves considerably different levels of effectiveness.

Compared to AutoFinanciering. nl's website, Sonze makes its buttons hard to find and gives its clickable elements little consistency in color.

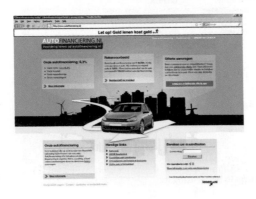

AutoFinanciering.nl applies a consistent color hue, varied in saturation and brightness levels, to different elements, helping the user better engage with the website.

AutoFinanciering.nl, on the other hand, highlights nearly every clickable item in a deep shade of red. Because the background is light in color, users can easily see the buttons.

On a content-rich website, where the color of content is constantly changing, using a neutral or accented background is sometimes best. This way, the content pops off the screen and doesn't compete with the background. Many photographers employ this technique on their portfolio websites to maintain focus on their pictures. Hulu, a popular video website, has an accented color scheme, as does COLOURlovers, our own website for creating and sharing color palettes.

Hulu accents its website in green to match its logo and uses few colors so that they don't compete with the content.

On COLOURlovers, we use a red accent to draw attention to the most important part of our website, the community section.

Color And Experience

Considering the cultural implications of the colors on your website is important, especially if you expect international traffic. Green, for instance, a popular color, is taken in Western society to mean environmental consciousness. In China, a green hat could imply that a man's wife is cheating on him. The color is sacred in the Islamic world, and it has significance in Catholicism. In some African countries, green represents the natural richness of Africa. It has also been associated with money, jealousy, growth, sickness, inexperience, evil, fertility, hope, youth and death.

The cyan in this palette doesn't fit any of the rules discussed above. But because little of it is used in this picture, it works beautifully.

This picture of sunset from Paulo Brandao's collection exemplifies how nature is a master of color[4].

Color affects people emotionally and psychologically, too. Faint tints of green are sometimes painted on the walls of patient rooms in asylums

4 http://www.flickr.com/photos/paulobrandao/2592581334/

because of its calming effect. Eating something from a green plate might give you the impression that it tastes bitter. A blue plate, however, might suppress your appetite, while a pink plate might make food seem sweeter[5].

By itself, this palette, taken from the plasma globe, is off-putting. But put in a context by the artist, just like the plasma globe, it can be a wonderful and beautiful range.

The plasma globe was an amazing invention by Nikola Tesla. Its colors are created simply by the excited charged particles of gas inside the globe[6].

All colors in the color wheel bring with them an equal number of interpretations, folklore tales and symbolic associations. So, there are really no rules or secret recipes for choosing colors. When it comes down to it, you just have to rely on what you think looks good and what you think is best for the project you're working on. Don't be afraid to sit back and see which color moves your heart, rather than your eyes, the most[6].

5   Maeyama, M. Apr 2001 The Color of Yummy, Parenting Volume 15 Issue 3.
6   http://www.flickr.com/photos/jurvetson/167197691/

Inspiration

"Good artists copy. Great artists steal" — Pablo Picasso

Color is in nature, science and everything human-made. It's everywhere. To get inspired, just look around. Probably within your arm's reach is a picture, piece of furniture, rusty car fender, flower or cat that has an interesting color composition. By picking out the colors from whatever you find, you'll probably be surprised by how easy it is to get inspired with color.

This fun palette from the picture of the candies would make any website look tasty.

We can find beautiful color palettes in pretty much everything. Once you have a palette to work with, arranging the colors in the right proportion is the next challenge. This image would be completely different if green were emphasized instead of pink[7].

We hope this chapter has given you a basic understanding of the core concepts of color theory, some terminology to help you talk about color and

7 http://www.flickr.com/photos/yomi955/783099682/

some ideas on where to find inspiration for your next creative project. This information will help you add some structure to your designs and help you use color to make an impact or improve the user experience or create a vibe. But what we hope most is that you feel inspired to play around with color. There are many "rules" about color usage, but rules are meant to be broken, and people should follow their heart and inspiration. Digital technology puts people only a few key strokes away from sharing their passions with everyone else, and when you have that big and diverse a market, there's more than enough room for everyone to be creative and unique and to create something beautiful. Good luck and happy coloring. ∎

At first, this picture of a curb may not seem to have much of a scheme, but when you start sampling colors from it, a nice palette is revealed. Though they may seem a bit incompatible, when toned down, pure color hues look great together.

Erosion is another of nature's tricks for creating beautiful palettes. http://www.flickr.com/photos/billselak/2491244618/

PERFORMANCE
OPTIMIZATION
for WEBSITES

Rene Schmidt

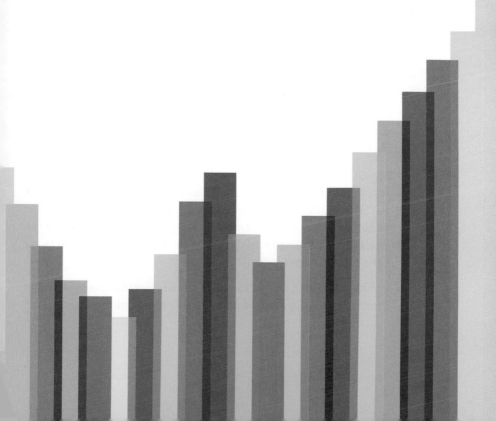

S low and unresponsive web sites are annoying. And if your website is annoying, your visitors are unlikely to buy goods or contact you. You lose money. Hence, it is important for you to optimize your website to provide a good user experience.

Yahoo's Firefox plug-in YSlow provides tips on how to make websites more responsive. We will not settle with just YSlow's tips, though, but take two further steps by optimizing MySQL and PHP as well. Let's go!

Tools You Will Need

- Your text editor of choice.

- A LAMP Web server (Linux, Apache or Lighttpd, MySQL, PHP5), configured.

- FTP access: FTP is a common way to access files on a Web server. Because this article is intended for Web designers and developers with some degree of knowledge, we will assume you already know how to access your files via FTP.

- SSH access: In order to change the configuration of a remote Web server running Linux, you will need to access your Web server via SSH using an SSH client such as Putty or Jellyfish. We will assume you know how to enter your SSH access information into an SSH client. Your Web host can provide SSH access information; that is, if your hosting plan includes SSH access and you have write permission to the Web server's configuration files, which may not be the case in a shared hosting environment.

- MySQL Tuning Primer: Please skip this part if you do not have write access to your MySQL configuration files or if your Web server does not run Linux or if you are not using a MySQL database. Otherwise, please go to *http://launchpad.net/mysql-tuning-primer/* and download the latest MySQL Tuning Primer script. Move it to your Web server using FTP or SSH. Do not run it just yet.

- Installing Smush.It for Firefox: this is a handy tool that gives you a huge shortcut with image optimization. Go to *http://smush.it/* and install

Smush.It for Firefox. It may interfere with Firefox' NoScript plug-in, so you may want to disable the latter temporarily.

- Installing Firebug and YSlow for Firefox: Yahoo's Firebug plug-in YSlow analyzes your website in a jiffy and provides real-world recommendations on how to achieve a more responsive website. Of course, we will not settle for YSlow's recommendations alone. But this is how you install YSlow:

- Download Firefox from *http://www.mozilla.org and install.*

- Start Firefox and install Firebug from *http://www.getfirebug.com*

- Install YSlow from *https://addons.mozilla.org/firefox/addon/5369.*

- Start analyzing your website right away. This is how you do it: restart Firefox and open your website. Go to "Tools > Firebug > Open Firebug". Then open the split window tab "YSlow" and click "Performance". YSlow will now analyze your website and show a performance grade. We are now going to boost that grade.

Give Correct Image Dimensions in IMG Tags

If you have an image in the dimensions of 2592 × 1944 pixels, and you would like to display it at 120x90, do not let browsers scale down the image:

```
<img src="img _ 2592x1944.png" width="130" height="90" alt="Bad" />
```

Transmitting the image would take a lot of time. Additionally, browsers would have to scale down the image on their own, which also takes time and does not look very good. Prepare all images first before putting them on the Web. A lot of free and powerful tools can help you scale down images: the GIMP and Paint.NET, for example.

The benefit: Better-looking images that can be transmitted more quickly, leading to a better user experience.

Reducing Image File Size

You will need to take care of every image file that you use on your website and see if it is possible to reduce the colour palette to 256 colours or even less. That, of course, depends on the image and file format. There are photos, line art, screenshots and so on, and every type needs special care. This is a tedious task, and nobody **wants to do it**.

Now, here is the shortcut: fire up Firefox and go to your website. At the bottom-right of your browser, you will see the stylized Smush.It head. Click it. A new browser tab will open. The Web service grabs your website's images and smushes them. Download the ZIP file provided and replace the images on your Web server with the optimized versions. Repeat for other pages on your website that have images.

The benefit: smaller image files contribute to faster loading times for your website, leading to a better user experience.

Sprites

Let's say you have a forum. In forums, people like to express their emotions using smiley faces. Because there are so many emotions, you would need many different smileys and thus many different image files, increasing the number of HTTP requests for each page delivered to the visitor. This can significantly slow down the loading time because there are many files to download.

Now imagine a 48 × 16 pixel image divided into three columns. In each column there is a 16 × 16 smiley: one with a sad face, one with a happy face, one with an angry face, etc. This single file that consists of three different images is a sprite. Using the CSS attribute "background-image" and "background-position", you can specify which cell to be displayed: for example, when to show a happy face on the page. That way, you can store all smiley faces in a single file, reducing the amount of HTTP requests big time. Naturally, the more images you aggregate into a sprite, the more you will benefit from this technique.

This method originates from the computer games industry and is suitable for images that do not need to be updated often: smileys, arrows, background images and bullet points, for example.

We would not recommend using this technique for images of text menu items, because you may have to change those from time to time and would thus have to change the sprite image every time and have to be careful not to break things. Head over to Smashing Magazine[1] for detailed information on this topic.

The benefit: fewer HTTP requests contribute to faster loading times for your website, leading to a better user experience.

Content Delivery Networks and Servers

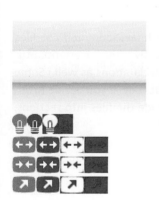

Sprites from Google's YouTube.

YSlow recommends putting static content, such as images, on a dedicated network of servers spread around the world so that images are stored in proximity to users. If you can afford renting servers all over the world, then please do follow this recommendation. For most users, this is not a feasible option because of the high costs. If at all, rent a dedicated server and set it up as a no-frills static content server without scripting or cookie support.

The benefit: better use of caches and an enhanced user experience, as well as lower traffic costs.

---

1   http://www.smashingmagazine.com/?p=6319/

Combine CSS and JavaScript

Reduce the amount of HTTP requests needed to transmit a Web page to the visitor's machine by aggregating all of your CSS files into one big CSS file and all your JavaScript files into one big JavaScript file. You can, of course, continue developing using multiple CSS and JavaScript files. You would then have to aggregate files for each development cycle.

Use either a text editor to aggregate files by hand, or, on Linux, go to your CSS directory and cat (short for "concatenate") them into one file via the SSH console:

```
cd your_css_directory
cat file1.css file2.css file3.css > file_to_link.css
```

and

```
cd your_javascript_directory
cat file1.js file2.js file3.js > file_to_link.js
```

The benefit: fewer HTTP requests contribute to faster loading times for your website, leading to a better user experience.

Take special care to maintain the order in which JavaScript and CSS files are loaded. This is important because CSS directives may overwrite others. (You may want to delete redundant CSS declarations as well.) Some JavaScript code may depend on other JavaScript code. If you decide to develop these aggregated files, make sure to divide the files into sections, using comments, for example:

```
/* Menu Styles */

(place menu styles here)

/* Header Styles */

(place menu styles here)
```

The benefit: fewer HTTP requests contribute to faster loading times for your website, leading to a better user experience.

Move CSS to the Top and JavaScript to the Bottom

Place CSS file requests in the <head></head> section of your HTML files, just as YSlow suggests. This way, browsers will already know how to display the page even before they get the HTML and will not need to realign objects during the loading process.

Place JavaScript files at the bottom, right above the closing <body> tag. This prevents JavaScript code from rendering the page while things are still being requested.

The benefit: the page loads as fast as possible, leading to a better user experience.

Minify CSS and JavaScript

First of all, many regular expression-based JavaScript compressors are prone to failure when the code to be compressed is flawed. Save yourself a lot of hassle and run your code through JSLint[2], and sort out any problems it may have detected. Even when your code passes JSLint, make sure your code is as close to perfect as possible, because even semicolons in strings make some compressors fail because the compressors mistake them for the end of a line.

In a text editor, copy your CSS or JavaScript onto the clipboard and paste it into the corresponding input field in Minify[3]. This incorporates Packer 3.1 and Minify[3], which provide very good minimizing performance. Then click "Hit me" and use the resulting CSS or JavaScript on your website. The more code you minify, the higher the performance gain, at least for JavaScript, because CSS cannot be minimized very much. Of course, other CSS and JavaScript compressors have even better compression ratios. You may want to try them as well.

2 http://www.jslint.com
3 http://www.reneschmidt.de/tools/minify/

YUICompressor, for example, has proven to be a good compromise between security, reliability and compression ratio. If you are using some kind of middleware, you may want to integrate YUICompressor to automate the processing of CSS and JavaScript files. Being a Java application, it can be integrated virtually anywhere.

The benefit: overall JavaScript performance can be significantly improved, leading to a better user experience, smaller files and lower traffic costs.

Make CSS and JavaScript External

Do not use inline CSS or JavaScript. Put all CSS and JavaScript into separate files. Not only is this more comprehensible (because you know where to look when you want to change something), but it also reduces the size of HTML files and takes advantage of caching (for example, when a JavaScript file or CSS file is used for more than one page). It also reduces the amount of HTTP requests.

The benefit: Better use of caches. Reloading content while browsing the website takes less time, leading to a better user experience.

Choose a Document Type

Choosing a document type does not have a direct impact on speed. However, by giving browsers clear and unambiguous rules on how to interpret HTML and CSS, you take full advantage of their potential.

Decide on one HTML or XHTML standard for all the pages on your website. HTML 4.0 is a good choice, although many website owners use XHTML 1.0 Transitional and seem to be happy with it. Do not omit a document type declaration anywhere and thus force browsers to guess which standard you are following. Instead, explicitly declare the document type in the first line of your HTML.

For XHTML 1.0 Transitional:

```
<!DOCTYPE html PUBLIC "-//W3C//DTD XHTML 1.0

Transitional//EN" "http://www.w3.org/TR/xhtml1/DTD/

xhtml1-transitional.dtd">
```

And for HTML 4.01 Transitional:

```
<!DOCTYPE HTML PUBLIC "-//W3C//DTD HTML 4.01

Transitional//EN" "http://www.w3.org/TR/html4/

loose.dtd">
```

The benefit: by telling browsers how they should handle your website, you take an important step in ensuring that your website looks consistent across different browsers.

Validate Your Pages

Especially when you offer Internet-related services, potential customers often carefully analyze your website to determine how important good quality is to you. A page that validates successfully on W3C's own validation service[4] suggests that you are dedicated to quality and that your pages are designed to look good in common Web browsers. Whether a valid page really is an indicator of your quality of service is another matter. But if a potential customer checks your website and finds that it does not validate, you probably have already lost her or him.

Do Not Use CSS Expressions

Web browsers that support CSS expressions let you put logic in CSS declarations. This is neither an accepted Web standard (and thus not supported by most Web browsers) nor good practice, because CSS is intended to separate program logic and content from document presentation. For

4 http://validator.w3.org/

example, when a document object is moved or updated, triggered by JavaScript or window resizing, the object's style needs to be updated for every step of the movement or update. CSS expressions take a lot more cycles to render than plain CSS, slowing down the process significantly. This is a waste of resources. Do not use CSS expressions. They are no good. They have never been accepted by the Web design community for a good reason. Even Microsoft, the "inventor" of CSS expressions, has ditched them in Internet Explorer 8.

Server Section

Now things get technical. You will require root-level access to your server machine. If you are in a shared-hosting environment, you may not have this level of access. This section will still be useful to you because you can check if your Web host's machine meets your requirements, and if it does not, you will know what to demand from your host.

Tuning a Web server requires low-level access to the machine, preferably via SSH. Therefore, you should have basic knowledge of how to log on using SSH, how to change configuration files as root and how to restart services. You probably will need to refer to your Web server's documentation from time to time to implement these tips. Explaining how exactly to do things in detail is impossible here because Web server software is heterogeneous. Things may get done differently depending on whether you use Debian GNU/Linux, Windows, Red Hat GNU/Linux, etc.

You probably will need to refer to your Web server's documentation from time to time to implement these tips.

We will assume a standard Debian GNU/Linux ("Lenny") as the server operating system here.

Apache: How to set up expires header

An "expires header" is an HTTP header attribute that indicates how long a file should be considered "fresh". Browsers do not request a file again as long as it is cached and has not expired, which reduces the number of HTTP requests.

Let's fix that. Log on to your Web server using SSH and become root:

```
su
```

Optionally, you may now install an easy-to-use text editor by issuing

```
aptitude install nano
```

at the command prompt. Let's continue by enabling Apache's expire module:

```
a2enmod expires
```

Make sure that parsing of .htaccess files is enabled. Edit your website's configuration file. The file name will vary. It should be located in "/etc/apache2/sites-enabled". Let's assume that the file name is "000-default" and that your preferred text editor is "nano":

```
nano /etc/apache2/sites-enabled/000-default
```

If "AllowOverride" has already been set to "All", leave it this way and quit. Otherwise, change "AllowOverride none" to "AllowOverride All". This is the most common setting. Save the file and exit. Then check Apache's configuration file:

```
apache2ctl -t
```

If everything went fine, restart and exit:

```
/etc/init.d/apache2 restart && exit
```

Then switch to your FTP or SCP client. Go to the wwwroot of your website and create a new file called ".htaccess". Notice the preceding dot. Load it in your desktop text editor, and enter the following lines:

```
ExpiresActive On

ExpiresDefault "access plus 1 year"

ExpiresByType text/html "access plus 1 hour"
```

This will make most files expire one year after being requested, while HTML pages will stay fresh for one hour. Rule of thumb: let static files stay fresh for a long time. You can experiment, setting different values for different content types, such as "text/javascript", "application/javascript", "text/css", "image/gif", "image/png", "image/jpg" and so on.

Use YSlow to check if the expires headers get set according to the new configuration. Clear your browser cache first.

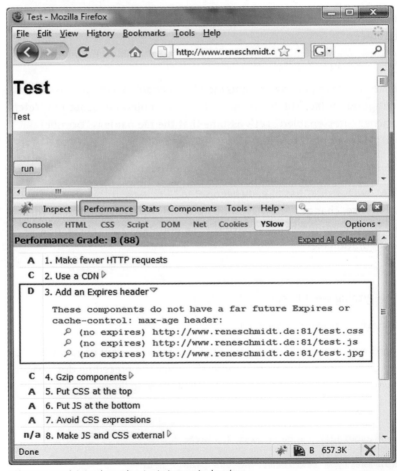

YSlow is complaining here about missing expire headers.

If you have set up expire headers, visitors to your website might still be using an old cached version of your CSS or JavaScript file, despite the fact that you had updated them before they expired. There is a simple work-around. Append a version parameter to the CSS and JavaScript links, like so:

```
<link rel="stylesheet" type="text/css" href="style.

css?v=1.0" />
```

Naturally, the parameter will not be read or processed anywhere. It serves merely as a indicator to browsers. When you change the file, simply up-date the parameter, for example, from "v=1.0" to "v=1.1", so that browsers fetch the updated version.

Lighttpd: How to set up expires header

Lighttpd, or Lighty, does not read .htaccess files. So, we have to put every-thing into Lighty's configuration files. Become root and go to /etc/light-tpd/conf-available:

```
su

cd /etc/lighttpd/conf-available
```

Create a new configuration file that accommodates the module's configuration.

```
nano ./01-expire.conf
```

For the sake of simplicity, we will set expire settings globally for all virtual hosts (vhosts). Put these lines into the newly created file:

```
server.modules += ( "mod_expire" )

$HTTP["url"] =~ "" {

  expire.url = ( "" => "access 12 hours" )
}

$HTTP["url"] =~ "(7z|rar|zip|gz|pdf|exe|css|js|png|gif|
jpg|ico)$" {
```

```
    expire.url = ( "" => "access 1 years" )
}
```

This configuration will push expire dates one year into the future for static files. Other content will expire one hour from being accessed. Save the file and exit. We now have to incorporate the new file into the current configuration and restart Lighty:

```
lighttpd-enable-mod expire
```

```
/etc/init.d/lighttpd force-reload
```

Apache: How to set up ETags

An ETag (short for "entity tag") is an HTTP response header used to determine changes in a given file's content. When a new HTTP response

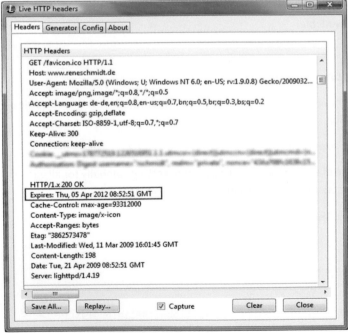

Lightly is now giving expire dates

contains the same ETag as an older HTTP response, their contents are considered to be the same without further downloading.

In Apache, file entity tags are set to "All". That means, an ETag is generated from the Inode, Mtime and file size information of a file. If your Web server does not provide ETags, you may have to enable them manually. Edit the .htaccess file of your website and search for "FileETag" directives. You may find something like "FileETag None". Change it to:

```
FileETag All
```

Save and upload the file. Then check whether Apache now provides ETags. If it does not, Apache may have been compiled with ETags disabled. You may have to switch to another Apache version or ask your Web host to enable this feature.

Lighttpd: How to set up ETags

Lighty on Debian defaults to ETags enabled, so no action is required. Nevertheless, this is how you would enable them. Become root:

```
su
```

```
cd /etc/lighttpd/conf-available
```

Create a new configuration file, in which we will enable ETags:

```
nano ./10-etags.conf
```

Put this line into the newly created file:

```
static-file.etags = !"enable"
```

Save the file and exit. Then make the new file current and restart Lighty:

```
lighttpd-enable-mod etags
```

```
/etc/init.d/lighttpd force-reload
```

Installing eAccelerator for PHP

Debian does not come with pre-built eAccelerator packages. We will have to compile them from source. We will assume your Web server has Debian Lenny and PHP 5 already up and running. We have to download some packages first:

```
aptitude install bzip2 php5-dev make
```

Become root and pull the source from the eAccelerator website:

```
su

cd /tmp

wget http://bart.eaccelerator.net/source\

/0.9.5.3/eaccelerator-0.9.5.3.tar.bz2
```

The current version as of March 2009 is 0.9.5.3. You may want to check for the latest version. Replace the version string accordingly.
Unpack the archive and change the directory:

```
tar xvjf eaccelerator-0.9.5.3.tar.bz2

cd eaccelerator-0.9.5.3
```

Start compiling right away:

```
export PHP_PREFIX="/usr"

$PHP_PREFIX/bin/phpize

./configure -enable-eaccelerator=shared \

-with-php-config=$PHP_PREFIX/bin/php-config

make && make install
```

eAccelerator's configuration file needs to be created manually:

```
nano /etc/php5/conf.d/ea.ini
```

Copy the following lines into the file and then save:

```
[eAccelerator]
extension="eaccelerator.so"
eaccelerator.shm_size="32"
eaccelerator.cache_dir="/tmp"
eaccelerator.enable="1"
eaccelerator.optimizer="1"
eaccelerator.check_mtime="1"
eaccelerator.debug="0"
eaccelerator.filter=""
eaccelerator.shm_max="0"
eaccelerator.shm_ttl="0"
eaccelerator.shm_prune_period="0"
```

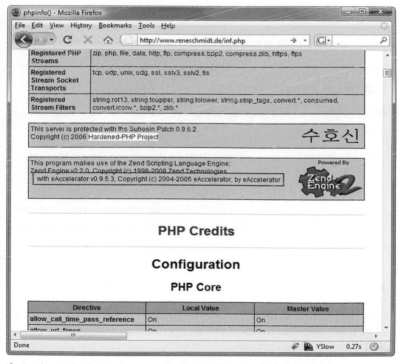

If eAccelerator has been set up correctly, there will be an extended copyright note.

```
eaccelerator.shm_only="0"
eaccelerator.compress="1"
eaccelerator.compress_level="9"
```

Depending on how your Web server incorporates PHP, you may have to restart:

```
/etc/init.d/lighttpd restart
```

or

```
/etc/init.d/apache2 restart
```

Let's check if eAccelerator has been compiled and installed successfully. Switch to your FTP or SCP client. Go to the wwwroot of your website and create a file called "inf.php". Put this line in it:

```
<?php phpinfo(); ?>
```

Save, close and upload the file. Go to your Web browser and request the file:

http://www.example.com/inf.php

Obviously, you will have to replace www.example.com with the actual host name.

Do not forget to remove packages that you do not need to run the server:

```
aptitude remove php5-dev make
```

Important: Remove inf.php if it is publicly accessible. It could provide useful information for hackers, and you certainly do not want to help them break into your system.

MySQL Tuning Primer

Once again, tuning MySQL requires SSH access. You will also need a MySQL account that is allowed to access runtime information ("root", for example, not to be confused with the server's root account) and an up-and-running MySQL server, of course. Log in using SSH and fetch

MySQL Tuning Primer:

```
wget http://launchpad.net/mysql-tuning-primer/trunk\
```

```
/1.5-r1/+download/tuning-primer.sh
```

Make it executable:

```
chmod +x ./tuning-primer.sh
```

You may need to resolve a dependency for the script. For its calculations, it relies on "bc", a small command-line calculator:

```
aptitude install bc
```

Launch the script and provide MySQL account information. MySQL Tuning Primer will now analyze runtime information and provide tips on optimizing your MySQL configuration.

Read these tips carefully and change MySQL's configuration accordingly:

```
nano /etc/mysql/my.conf
```

For example, if Tuning Primer suggests that "Your query_cache_size seems to be too high. Perhaps you can use these resources elsewhere", then edit the configuration file as stated above. Search for "query_cache_size" and lower its value by roughly 10%. Do not change configuration values too much in one shot, but rather do it in 10 to 20% increments. Save and exit.

Restart MySQL:

```
/etc/init.d/mysql restart
```

We recommend waiting 48 hours before starting another tuning session to let MySQL accumulate meaningful statistics.

Enabling Transparent Compression

If you run a low-traffic website, with either few visitors or small HTML, CSS and JavaScript files, compressing files may not be feasible, because compressing on the fly means that an additional load could push your server over the edge when it has to cope with a critical load level.

However, if you do have left-over resources and large text files (such as HTML, CSS, JavaScript and JSON), you may want to enable compressing, because it can save bandwidth and reduce transmission times.

Enabling compression for Apache

This is how you enable compression for Apache. Become root and edit deflate.conf

```
su
```

```
nano /etc/apache2/mods-available/deflate.conf
```

By default, mod_deflate for Apache in Debian Lenny will apply compression for three content types: "text/html", "text/plain" and "text/xml". But this is insufficient. You may want to extend the list of content types to include CSS, JavaScript and maybe even JSON, ATOM and RSS as well. Deflate.conf should then look like this:

```
<IfModule mod_deflate.c>
    AddOutputFilterByType DEFLATE text/html
    AddOutputFilterByType DEFLATE text/plain
    AddOutputFilterByType DEFLATE text/xml
    AddOutputFilterByType DEFLATE text/css
    AddOutputFilterByType DEFLATE text/javascript
    AddOutputFilterByType DEFLATE application/xhtml+xml
    AddOutputFilterByType DEFLATE application/javascript
    AddOutputFilterByType DEFLATE application/
    x-javascript
    AddOutputFilterByType DEFLATE application/json
    AddOutputFilterByType DEFLATE text/json
    AddOutputFilterByType DEFLATE application/xml
    AddOutputFilterByType DEFLATE application/rss+xml
    AddOutputFilterByType DEFLATE application/rdf+xml
    AddOutputFilterByType DEFLATE application/atom+xml
# Netscape 4.x has some problems...

BrowserMatch ^Mozilla/4 gzip-only-text/html
```

```
# Netscape 4.06-4.08 have some more problems

BrowserMatch ^Mozilla/4\.0[678] no-gzip

# MSIE masquerades as Netscape, but it is fine

BrowserMatch \bMSIE !no-gzip !gzip-only-text/html

</IfModule>
```

Commented lines have been taken from the official mod_deflate documentation.

You may be tempted to enable compression globally for all file types, because browsers tend not to request (or accept) content encoding for images. Practically speaking, serious issues could arise when browsers request compressed content for large files that are already compressed, possibly leading to a DDOS-type situation. This is why we have left out images, video and other such content types, because these files are usually already compressed, and even if browsers do request them compressed (due to an error or hacking), the Web server will not compress them.

Enabling compression for Lighttpd

Compression is enabled by default in Lighttpd for Debian Lenny, so there should be no need to enable it manually. Even so, knowing how to enable compression might come in handy in future.

Become root and go to /etc/lighttpd/conf-available:

```
su

cd /etc/lighttpd/conf-available
```

Create a new configuration file, in which we will enable the module:

```
nano ./05-compress.conf
```

Put the following line in the newly created file:

```
server.modules += ( "mod_compress" )
```

Save the file and exit. Incorporate the new file into the current configuration and restart Lighty:

```
lighttpd-enable-mod compress
```

```
/etc/init.d/lighttpd force-reload
```

Enabling compression for PHP

You may want to enable transparent output compression for PHP scripts as well. Become root by issuing "su". Then edit php.ini. The path depends on which Web server you are using and how it incorporates PHP. For Apache and mod_php, it would be:

```
nano /etc/php5/apache2/php.ini
```

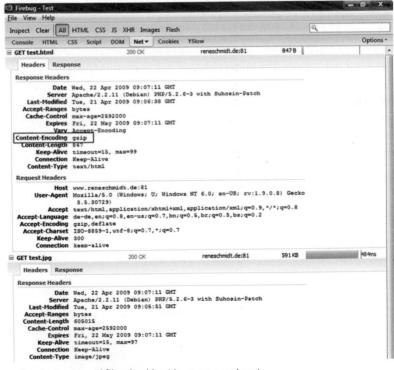

Already compressed files should not be compressed again.

For Lighttpd and FastCGI, it would be:

```
nano /etc/php5/cgi/php.ini
```

Search for "zlib.output_compression" and enable it:

```
zlib.output_compression = On
```

Save and exit. Restart the Web server by either

```
/etc/init.d/lighttpd restart
```

or

```
/etc/init.d/apache2 restart
```

Verifying compression
Once again, go to Firebug's Net tab and reload your website. HTML, Java-Script, CSS, XML, RSS, ATOM, JSON and plain text content should now be compressed by default, while everything else should not be.

Avoid Redirects When Possible

Websites that have evolved over time often have many redirects. Files get moved, become obsolete and vanish. Redirecting requests for files that have moved or vanished is a good idea because it helps users find what they are searching for. If you install redirects, check whether there is already a redirection chain:

A → B → C → D

In this example, a visitor is requesting file A. The request gets redirected to destination B, then C, then D. This makes for four requests, when two would suffice:

A → D

The benefit: if you carefully optimize redirection chains, your Web server will be able to serve more visitors at once.

How Do You Detect Longer-Than-Necessary Redirection Chains?

Switch to Firefox. Bring up Firebug, and click the Net tab. If disabled, check "Network monitoring" and apply settings. Firebug will then reload the current page and list every request necessary to load the current page.

When a visitor requests an HTML file, Firebug will list every request along with its response code. 302 means a temporary redirect. This example server is not optimized, so you cannot compare absolute numbers with real-world production servers. In this case, four requests take 180 milliseconds to process. This can add up to seconds if a page request leads to more than one long redirection chain. Instead of redirecting indirectly (in an .htaccess file, for example), like so:

```
Redirect /A.html http://www.example.com/B.html

Redirect /B.html http://www.example.com/C.html

Redirect /C.html http://www.example.com/D.html
```

you should let visitors take the direct path:

```
Redirect /A.html http://www.example.com/D.html
```

A short redirection chain can be processed significantly more quickly than a long chain. In this case, it took 105 milliseconds to redirect the visitor.

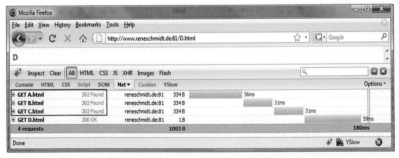

Avoid unnecessary redirects.

Link Consistently

With permalinks enabled, WordPress automatically redirects URLs without a trailing slash:

```
http://www.example.com/post -> http://www.example.com/post/
```

Note the trailing slash. This creates two requests, when one would suffice. Make sure, then, that WordPress permalinks have a trailing slash, which reduces the number of requests necessary to serve a visitor. In other words, if you link internally, make sure the links always have a trailing slash; unless you link to static files, such as *.html or *.php, that is.

By the way, two links should not serve the same content. Make sure that requests to http://www.example.com/postname actually do get redirected to *http://www.example.com/postname*, not for performance purposes but rather for search engine optimization, because doubled content could lead to ranking penalties.

Avoid Dead Links

Please be careful about this: if a non-existent file is requested, the server must send a 404 header to explicitly tell the client that this file is gone. As a website owner, you should make sure not to link to non-existent HTML, CSS and JavaScript files. Many Web servers log 404 requests in separate log files, and so many (avoidable) 404 requests will bloat your log files, which in turn raises the required server resources (such as CPU cycles and disk space).

How Do You Detect Dead Internal Links?

This is a walk in the park. Let's assume you have an almost-white background image called "background.png" that you assign via the CSS attribute "background-image" to the body tag:

```
body { background-image: url("background.png"); }
```

Let us further assume that the file does not exist. By looking at the Web page, you would not notice the missing background; or at least browsers usually do not explicitly report missing files that are to be loaded via CSS. Switch to Firefox. Clear the browser's cache. Bring up Firebug and reload the current page. Firebug will list all requests, including those that come from CSS declarations.

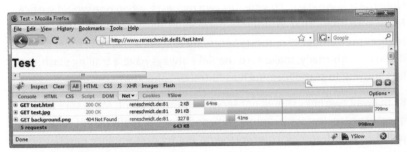

Firebug highlights requests that have led to a 404 response.

Firebug highlights requests that have led to a 404 response. Correct this issue by either putting the right file in the right place or by changing or removing the CSS declaration. This way, you use the server's resources more efficiently.

New Kid On The Block: Page Speed by Google

Page Speed is a tool that Google has been using internally to improve the performance of its Web applications. It's a Firefox add-on integrated with Firebug, just like YSlow.

While both plug-ins have many similarities, Page Speed provides information that YSlow does not offer:

- JavaScript events,
- Display of unused CSS declarations,
- Display of inefficient CSS selectors.

This plug-in is obviously heavily geared to large Web applications that would benefit from such fine-grained optimization. If you are a Web application developer, give it a try. ∎

Dmitry Fadeyev

Design to

SELL

Increasing Conversion Rates

Every website owner wants their website to perform well, whether that means getting more sales, sign-ups or RSS subscribers. The question is, how do you convert a new visitor into a loyal customer? This chapter looks at the theory of how to sell effectively and lists practical techniques to help you boost conversion rates.

Most websites are not works of art or things made to be appreciated solely for their beauty or expression. Websites are functional interfaces that serve a specific purpose. If you run an online store, the purpose of your website is to sell goods. If you run a Web application, your website is there to get people to sign up. Whatever industry you operate in and whatever type of business, organization or community you run, you want your website to perform by getting those sales, sign-ups, subscribers or clicks.

"Conversion" is an online marketing term that describes an instance of a visitor to your website performing an action that you deem to be desirable. For example, if you run an online store, one likely conversion would be the sale of a product; in the case of a blog, a conversion might be a subscription to your RSS feed. Conversions are tracked using a conversion rate: the ratio of all visitors to your website to the number of visitors who perform the desired action.

> Most website owners want a high conversion rate. The question is, how do you turn a new visitor of your website into a loyal customer?

Most website owners want a high conversion rate. The question is, how do you turn a new visitor of your website into a loyal customer? To answer this, let's look at what it takes to sell effectively.

What Sells?

To sell effectively, you have to sell solutions, not products. You also have to sell benefits, not features. Your customers aren't looking for products, services or features: they're looking for solutions to their specific problems. Features are just the things that make up your product or service, but benefits are what people get from using your product; they are the reason for choosing your product. For example, saying that the iPod Nano has

16 gigabytes of space tells me a lot about its technical specifications and little about its benefits; but saying that it holds 4,000 songs clearly highlights the benefit that storage capacity gives me. This in turn solves my need to carry my entire music library in my pocket.

Once you know what you're selling (that is, your product's solutions and benefits) you need to break down the barriers that customers will put up when evaluating how valuable your product is to them. These barriers are their reasons why they shouldn't buy your product. These barriers will range from the really strong (they may simply hate your product or don't have nearly the budget to buy it) to the weak (maybe they don't see the feature they need or think it's expensive or don't like the color).

> You need to break down the barriers that customers will put up when evaluating how valuable your product is to them.

These barriers can be tackled directly and hopefully broken down. For example, if the product seems expensive to potential customers, highlight the value it will give them by pointing out the amount of money, time or stress they'll save by using it.

Lack of features can often be tackled by talking about simple workarounds; after all, your customers are looking not for features but for solutions to their problems, and so if you can tell them how they can solve their problem using your product (perhaps by using different features than the ones they had in mind), you can break down those barriers.

AIDA

One very popular approach to sales is called AIDA, which stands for "Attention, Interest, Desire, Action". AIDA is a guide to structuring your sales pitch. In any sales pitch, the goal is to close the sale, and your approach should maximize the effectiveness of the pitch so that when you get to the end, the prospective buyer wants the product enough to say "Yes". Just like with a standard sales pitch, AIDA can be used in a conversion funnel on the Web, where the website, instead of the salesperson, plays the key role in selling.

The first stage in the AIDA pitch is "Attention". This is especially important for websites because of the speed with which potential customers could navigate away from your website. You have just a brief moment to grab their attention, and you have to keep it long enough to close the sale. That first moment is absolutely critical because the rest of the pitch will be useless if your potential customer leaves now. Grab attention by making a strong claim that your

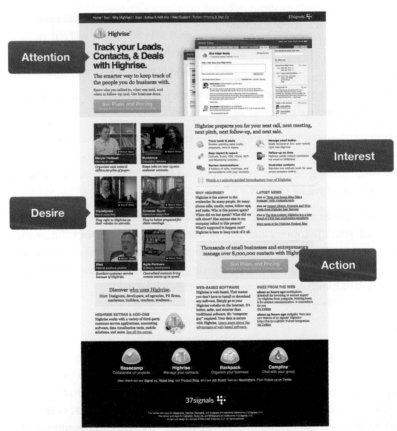

The Highrise website from 37signals uses the AIDA approach to maximize conversions. First, they grab your attention with a very concise product summary and benefit claim: "The smarter way to keep track of the people you do business with". Interest is built with a list of benefits. Videos of clients talking about how Highrise helps them run their business help generate desire. Finally, a large call-to-action button invites you to see the pricing plans.

solution will clearly improve the lives of your visitors. Make it concise and punchy, and make it clear why your visitors should care.

The next two stages, "Interest" and "Desire", are the part that sells the product. If you've made a claim in the "Attention" stage, now is the time to back it up. Clearly and concisely explain what your product does and how it will give your visitors real value. Create desire by talking about the benefits your product will bring to customers. If you can paint a vivid picture so that visitors can imagine using your product and enjoying its benefits, their desire for your product will grow.

The final step is a call to "Action". If you're selling a tangible product, invite the customer to buy it and tell them how they can pay for it. If the product is a Web app or service, invite the visitor to sign up. At this stage, you have to close the sale, so the call to action is absolutely vital. People who are willing to buy just need that last bit of direction on how to pay or sign up, and people who are sitting on the fence need that last little push.

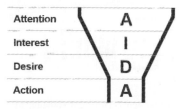

The AIDA sales funnel.

Recently, the letter "S", which stands for "Satisfaction", was added to AIDA, forming AIDAS. Getting customers is great, but getting those customers to return or tell their friends about your product is even better. You do this by making sure they are satisfied with the service. It doesn't mean your service or product needs to be perfect; it does mean you should provide great customer service. Solving customer service problems is a great way to build loyal customers because it shows that your company can be relied on even when things don't go as planned.

Show The Product

If you were shopping at a real bricks-and-mortar store, you would be able not only to see the products but to touch and try them. Seeing an actual product before buying it gives you a lot more information about it. You get a good feel for what you're purchasing.

When shopping online, however, we're limited by the amount and kind of information we can get, and so it's surprising that some websites don't even show what their products look like.

Even if you sell digital goods, such as desktop or Web applications, showing screenshots – or, even better, videos – is essential. When people see what a product looks like, they can begin to imagine using that product. This is important. If you can get your potential customer to imagine using your product, you will begin to create in them a desire to own it. What's more, good-looking interfaces aren't simply attractive, they are perceived as being more usable[1].

Apple displays large screenshots of Numbers, its spreadsheet application, right at the top of the page.

Use Video To Showcase The Product

Video is becoming a very popular medium to showcase products online, especially digital goods like desktop and Web applications. This is because you can usually show a lot more in a video in a shorter period of time than you can with screenshots and text. Video also takes less effort to digest because all you have to do is watch and listen.

1 "Apparent Usability vs. Inherent Usability: Experimental Analysis on the Determinants of the Apparent Usability", by Masaaki Kurosu and Kaori Kashimura, CHI '95 Conference Companion, 1995, p. 292–293

A great way to use video to show off your product is by embedding it in a prominent position on your landing page. It may be helpful to prepare a script beforehand and then narrate over top of your previously recorded session to ensure that the audio is clear and without mistakes. Keep the script brief and to the point.

The AIDA structure may come in handy here, because you would first talk about what problem your product solves, how your product solves it and what benefits one gets from using your product, and then you would invite the viewer to sign up or continue browsing the website to learn more.

Scannable Feature Lists

If you're selling a product or service, you probably have a list of features to advertise. You want to get people to read and digest this list. The problem is, lists are boring, and they're especially boring when they have a lot of text. People browsing your website certainly won't put much effort into reading your ads – they're there to browse, not work – so it's up to you to make the list as easy to process as possible. Thankfully, there are a few easy things you can do to make that happen.

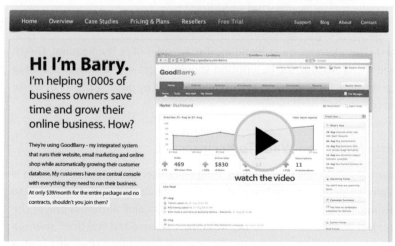

GoodBarry opens its landing page with a large embedded screencast video. The large play button and call to action ("watch the video") invite visitors to click on it.

First of all, use icons or images. Icons beside feature descriptions in lists work like bullet points: they're little anchors on the page on which our eyes can easily focus. Icons and images also look more interesting than text and so will more likely attract the eye than words.

Secondly, use short headings for each feature. These should be only a few words so that they're as quick to process as the icons. Their contrast with the background should be stronger and their font larger than those of the description – again, to grab attention. Provide a more detailed description underneath each heading, set in a smaller font and with lighter con-

Track leads & deals
Monitor pending sales leads, proposals, wins & losses.

Easy import & export
Outlook, Excel, CSV, vCard, ACT! and Basecamp contacts.

Review conversations
A history of calls, meetings, and conversations with your contacts.

Manage email better
Easily forward or bcc: your emails right into Highrise.

Follow-up on time
Highrise sends instant reminders via email or SMS/text.

Centralize contacts
Maintain one address book for your entire company online.

Highrise makes the feature list on its website scannable by using icons, contrast and white space. Also, note the benefits stated in each heading

trast. This element must blend in; if the reader likes the heading, they'll read the blurb, but the description shouldn't get in the way of scanning the whole list. Lastly, make the list easy to scan by putting plenty of white space between each item.

Gifts Make You Want To Reciprocate

Another great sales technique to bring you closer to a sale or conversion is to give something for nothing. When you receive a gift, you feel a need to reciprocate, to give something back. Robert Cialdini, author of one of the greatest books about influence, "Influence: Science and Practice[2]",shares a few examples of how gifts can help you sell. Receiving a small gift from a

2   Cialdini, R., Influence: Science and Practice, 5th ed., (Allyn & Bacon 2008).

Linkscape

A professional quality inlink tool that uses patented SEOmoz metrics. Inlinks, anchor text distribution and more. Linkscape's metrics are also available in the Site Intelligence Service API.

FREE!

Trifecta

Measures metrics to estimate the relative popularity and importance of Page, Blog or Domain. Trifecta replaces SEOmoz's Page Strength tool.

FREE!

Term Target

Helps determine how targeted a particular page is for a specified keyword by analyzing a variety of factors.

FREE!

Backlink Analysis Tool

Get an advanced look at the keywords websites are linking to you with.

SEOmoz Firefox Toolbar

The power of Linkscape is now available inside Firefox with the SEOmoz Toolbar.

FREE!

SEOmoz Labs

SEOmoz Labs is a place where our more adventurous PRO users can check out the *bleeding edge* of SEOmoz technology and product design.

SEOmoz provides commercial tools for SEO professionals, but it also gives out a lot of smaller tools for free. This is a great way to attract traffic and capitalize on the reciprocation phenomenon.

stranger made people twice as likely to buy raffle tickets from them. People were more inclined to fill out a survey if they were given a $5 gift check right away than if they were promised a $50 reward upon completion. Giving sweets with bills at restaurants increased the value of tips.

So, what can you give away for free on your site that will make people want to reciprocate? If you sell software, how about giving away a 30-day trial? Maybe release a portion of your product completely free of charge through what's called a "freemium" model, in which customers can use a basic version of your product for free but have to pay for additional features? Some website owners build small tools and release them free of charge to all visitors; for example, 37signals offers a couple of small applications called Tadalist and Writeboard, which complement its commercial offerings, free of charge. Giving those applications away for free makes people more likely to try out and buy its other offerings.

Social Proof

Social proof is a psychological phenomenon that occurs when people aren't sure about the course of action they should take and so do what everyone else does. For example, an experiment was conducted in which several people would look up at the sky. Many bystanders noticed this and would also look up to see what the others were looking at. Indeed, it was so effective that the experiment had to be aborted at one point when it began to impede traffic.

People feel safer and more reassured following others. If they see others buying a product, they feel safer purchasing it because they know it's popular. It must be pretty good, right? We can use social proof to help boost conversions for popular products and services by advertising that they're popular or that others have approved of them. For example, user reviews are a great way to recommend products. Amazon does something similar with its "Customers who bought this item also bought these" section, which recommends items based on other people's purchasing behavior.

Logitech V220 Cordless Optical Mouse for Notebooks (Dark Silver) ★★★★☆ (173) $24.99

Toshiba Satellite A305-S6908 15.4-Inch Laptop ★★★★☆ (46) $849.84

Logitech Optical Notebook Mouse Plus (USB) ★★★★☆ (195) $13.23

Kingston DataTraveler 4 GB USB 2.0 Flash Drive DTI / 4GB ★★★★★ (685) $10.93

Toshiba Satellite L305-S5924 15.4-Inch Laptop ★★★★☆ (20) $519.99

Amazon recommends products that buyers of the same product also bought. Amazon also lets customers review products, making good use of the social proof phenomenon.

Subliminal Suggestion

Images and objects also play a part in influencing behavior. A study found that showing children a Santa Claus hat increased the likelihood that they would share candy with other children. Exposing kids to the Toys 'R' Us logo yielded the opposite effect, making sharing less likely. This is because people make associations with certain images and objects, and by exposing people to carefully selected visuals, you can condition them to perform the behavior you want.

You can use this idea when designing your website. Don't simply choose images for their decorative value; instead, think about what emotions you want your visitors to experience. What message do you want your images to communicate? Select images that have meaning and will help put your visitors in the right frame of mind about your product.

Always Provide Next Actions

When should you close a sale? Simple: ABC. "Always be closing". You will convert visitors into customers at different stages in the process and at different speeds, so by delaying closing the sale, you risk dragging those people who have already made up their mind through more marketing, when all they really want to do is sign up. Provide easy access to that purchase, sign-up or subscription link on every page of your website, and perhaps in multiple places. Of course, don't flood the page with calls to action; just provide enough closure opportunities to make it easy for people who have made up their mind and want to sign up to do so.

Legacy Locker display a photo of a happy family next to its introduction to elicit a desire in visitors to care for and protect their loved ones.

You should also aim to keep the process flowing. This means leaving no dead ends. For example, when the visitor gets to the bottom of a marketing blurb or description, where do they go next? Provide links to next actions right at the bottom of each section and sub-section. Make it easy for visitors to browse by directing them through the sales funnel rather than leaving them to figure out where they should go. This can be done by putting links with labels such as "Learn more" at the bottom of brief descriptions and adding call-to-action buttons like "Buy now" or "Take the tour" right under your main copy. Make sure the visitor always knows where to go next, so that when they finish reading a section, a link is waiting to direct them to the next stage in the process.

Use Scarcity To Drive Demand

When a limited amount of goods is available and those goods have value, getting ahold of one give its owner a certain privilege. This is because once

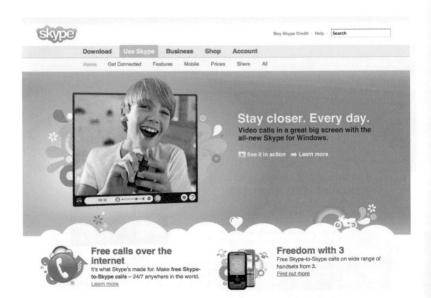

Skype leaves no dead ends. Notice how under each little feature description is one or more next-action links, like "Learn more" or "See it in action".

the item is sold out, purchasing it becomes much more difficult, and so its value grows. Google generated a lot of buzz through scarcity when it first launched Gmail, its Web-based email application. It did this by limiting access to the beta: you could only get it if you were invited by someone who already had an account. Getting a Gmail account was a privilege, then, and people in turn wanted it more than they would have if it was completely open to new sign-ups.

Scarcity also makes people think that if they delay, they might miss their chance to get the product, and so they will act quickly. Advertising limited-time offers and limited stocks are great ways to push people who are sitting on the fence into making the purchase or signing up.

Money-Back Guarantee To Eliminate Risk

Risk is one of the biggest barriers to conversions. Can people trust your company? What if your product doesn't do what they want? What if they discover something better? Risk sows seeds of doubt in the minds of visitors. They're not sure whether to buy your product or sign up for your service because there are too many unknowns. Thankfully, we have a good deal of control over risk, and the best way to tackle risk is to offer a money-back guarantee.

Instead of displaying the standard "In stock" label, Overclockers shows the exact number of goods in stock when the level is low. This pushes people who want the item to make the purchase quickly, because if they don't do it now, they might be too late.

Money-back guarantees mean just that: if the customer isn't happy, they send the product back and get their money refunded, usually in a limited timeframe, such as 30 days. Money-back guarantees shouldn't scare you, because if your product is good, you will likely see few returns. Money-back guarantees may even be cheaper for your business, because if you don't offer one and a customer really wants his money back, he can get his bank to refund his money, and then you'll get a chargeback, which means you'll pay an additional fee on top of the money you refund. Offering a money-back guarantee means no chargeback fees, more customers (because of the lower risk) and higher trust in your business.

Let People Try It

One of the best ways to sell your product is to get people to try it out. When people try a product, they are doing more than just looking at it or considering it: they are actually using it, which means they are getting involved. They start to experience it, learn how it works and maybe even

Who Should Read This Book?

If you're working on the Web today, you need a copy of this book to understand exactly why some designs work, while others don't. It covers graphic design principles in a very straightforward and easy-to-follow way: you don't need to have had any formal art or design training to benefit from this book.

No-risk Money-back Guarantee

Of course we're *so confident* that you'll treasure this book for years to come that we're happy, as always, for you to try it risk-free for 30 days. If you purchase a copy of *The Principles of Beautiful Web Design* and you think it fails to be everything you wanted, we would like you to have your money back.

Simply contact us and we will see to it that you receive a prompt and courteous refund of the full purchase price minus shipping and handling.

What could be fairer than this?

Sitepoint offers a 30-day money-back guarantee for its books, which means customers face very little risk: if they're not happy with the product, they can get their money back.

put their own data into it if it's a software application. Essentially, they become much more involved with the product, and so the chance that they buy it grows dramatically.

If you sell a digital product, such as a desktop or Web application, why not let people try it? Many applications offer online demos in which people can log in and play around without any commitment. Many also use the Freemium model, in which people can use a basic version of the product free of charge but have to pay for extra features. This is great because users start to do two things: they learn how the product works, and they save their data in it. Freemium users invest their time in your product, so they're inclined to stick with it when they need more features, making a premium upgrade likely. Another way to let people try your product is through a limited-time trial.

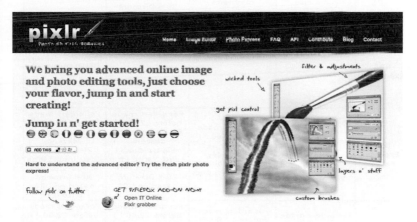

Pixlr, a Web-based image editing application, gives you a demo link right on the landing page. Clicking on it lets you instantly try out the product without having to sign up or divulge any personal information.

Don't Push Customers Away With Shipping Costs

A study by ForeSee Results[3], analyzing 10,500 transactions in 30 online stores, discovered that the deciding factor that closed the deal for 34% of users was that the stores didn't charge shipping costs. People like to know

3   http://www.foreseeresults.com/Thank_Top100_Mayo8.html

that the price they see in their shopping cart is the same amount they'll get charged on their credit cards. The last thing they want to see is additional costs at the end of the check-out process.

Offering free delivery would surely boost sales, but it may not be a viable option for every store. If you do charge a shipping cost, be transparent about it and offer clear and simple shipping options. At this stage, you don't want to confuse potential customers about how much money they'll

Delivery conditions				
Type of delivery	Germany	EU	within Europa	outside Europa
UPS Standard	For orders made before 12.00 *) Delivery within 3-5 working days to centers of commerce 6,50 € (from 200,- € free of charge **)	For orders made before 12.00 *) Delivery within 3-5 working days to centers of commerce 30% Discount based on UPS price list	For orders made before 12.00 *) Economic delivery Optimum transit time ***) 30% Discount based on UPS price list	
UPS Expedited				For orders made before 12.00 *) Economic delivery Optimum transit time ***) 30% Discount based on UPS price list
UPS Express Saver	For orders made before 12.00 *) Delivery by next working day before 12.00 30% Discount based on UPS price list	For orders made before 12.00 *) Delivery by next working day 30% Discount based on UPS price list	For orders made before 12.00 *) Fast economical delivery. Please check exact transit time at www.ups.com 30% Discount based on UPS price list	For orders made before 12.00 *) Fast economical delivery. Please check exact transit time at www.ups.com 30% Discount based on UPS price list
UPS Express	For orders made before 12.00 *) Delivery by next working day before 10.30**) 30% Discount based on UPS price list	For orders made before 12.00 *) Delivery by next working day before 12.00 to centers of commerce 30% Discount based on UPS price list	For orders made before 12.00 *) Fast economic delivery. Please check exact transit time at www.ups.com 30% Discount based on UPS price list	For orders made before 12.00 *) Fast economic delivery. Please check exact transit time at www.ups.com 30% Discount based on UPS price list
UPS Express Plus	For orders made before 12.00 *) Delivery by next working day before 8.30 **)	For orders made before 12.00 *) Delivery by next working day before 9.00 to centers of commerce		

Shipping option hell at Badgepoint. Don't force your users to analyze large cryptic spreadsheets. Offer simple and clear shipping solutions instead.

be charged: it should be clear. A good way to do this is to update the total cost on the check-out page when the user selects a shipping method, so that the total reflects the full price. You should also make the options clear and easy to select, because you don't want to slow down customers in the check-out process.

Eliminate Choice Paralysis

There is a concept in marketing called choice paralysis. It describes the state of consumers when presented with too many choices of the same type and few differentiating factors. For example, when you go to the supermarket and look at the shelves of pasta, you will probably see a lot of brands, each offering different pasta shapes in different packages. Which do you pick? Which is better? Which one do you like best? When the choices are too many, you become paralyzed: you don't know which product to pick. Choice paralysis doesn't just delay purchases; it can also cause buyer's remorse. More choice means more stuff to look through and more reasons to regret not buying something else if they end up disliking your product. To help combat choice paralysis, keep your product selection small and well differentiated. If you still offer too many choices and can't reduce them any further, recommend one of them to your visitors, such as your most popular product or service plan.

Highrise effectively uses visuals to make the service plan it recommends stand out.

Use visuals to highlight that choice and make it stand out from the rest. People who are unsure about what they want will have an easier time and feel safer going with what's recommended, and those who are sure can easily pick any other product that suits their needs.

The Gutenberg Rule

The Gutenberg diagram (or Gutenberg rule) is a map of something called "reading gravity". Reading gravity is the path our eyes tend to follow when we read a page of text, which in the Western world is left to right and top to bottom.

The Gutenberg diagram is split into four areas:

- the Primary Optical area in the top-left
- the Strong Fallow area in the top-right
- the Weak Fallow area in the bottom-left
- the Terminal area in the bottom-right.

The Gutenberg rule tells us that the reader will most likely start looking at the top-left corner of the page and end up in the bottom-right. It also tells us that the bottom-left area gets the least attention.

BusinessCatalyst uses the Gutenberg principle to lay out the introductory text and call to action, "Watch the video", on its landing page. An arrow helps guide visitors to the button.

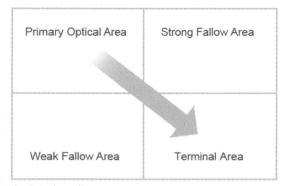

Primary Optical Area	Strong Fallow Area
Weak Fallow Area	Terminal Area

The Gutenberg diagram.

We can use this idea in Web design by placing key information in the top-left area and positioning a call-to-action button or link in the bottom-right terminal area, where a casual visitor will likely end up looking after a quick glance at the page. Note that the Gutenberg principle works best on pages with a balanced distribution of content. So, if certain elements on your page have strong contrast and eye-catching colors, they will likely attract the visitor's gaze, even if they lie in weaker areas.

Footnotes

Sometimes you need to mention detailed technical specifications or perhaps special requirements (for example, the minimum requirements to run a piece of software). You could mention these things in the marketing copy, but that would probably break the flow. These details usually do not help sell your product, because they are simply extra information and not content that highlights benefits. You can improve your copy by moving this information to footnotes.

Your copy will be slimmer and more focused on conversions, while the footnotes with extra information will be available if and when the reader needs them. Make sure to use footnotes for good and not evil, though. Don't state something in the main copy and then contradict it in a footnote: for example, saying that a product or deal is free when it really isn't. Not everyone reads footnotes, so being honest about what you offer is best. Make sure you don't deceive visitors or give them inaccurate expectations; that ultimately leads to dissatisfied customers.

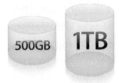

Room for it all.
Time Capsule is your one place for backing up everything. Its massive 500GB or 1TB server-grade hard drive gives you all the capacity and safety you need. So whether you have 250 songs or 250,000 songs to back up, room is the last thing you'll run out of. And considering all that storage and protection come packaged in a high-speed Wi-Fi base station starting at $299, data isn't the only thing you're saving.

*1GB = 1 billion bytes and 1TB = 1 trillion bytes; actual formatted capacity less.

This footnote on Apple's website explains storage capacities.

Make It Easy To Sign Up

Sign-up forms are barriers. Nobody likes filling them out because they take time and effort. The sign-up form is probably the last stage in your conversion funnel, so make sure you lose as few people as possible by making the form short and simple. Don't ask for optional information; it can always be filled in later. Keep the form slim to make it quick and painless to fill in. It's also helpful to remove additional navigation and content elements from the sign-up page and leave just the form and a link back to the home page. This way, there is little to distract the user from filling out the form.

With many online forms, the user realizes they have made a mistake only after they have submitted the form. They wind up back on the same page

Posterous has a unique process: you don't even have to sign up. All you do to start a new blog is send an email with your first post.

and face a list of things to change or fill in. Save users that trip by validating each field with AJAX as they fill it out. Place error messages right beside their respective fields. That way, if the users make a mistake, they can fix it before submitting the form.

Conclusion

We've looked at the theory of selling effectively: selling solutions instead of products, and selling benefits instead of features. We've looked at how the popular AIDA sales pitch structure can be adapted to the Web. We've also looked at practical techniques for boosting the conversion rate of your website.

Most websites are not art. They're not built to be appreciated simply for their design. Instead, they are meant to perform a specific task, such as sell a product or present blog articles to readers. The design of your website should work towards achieving its goal. The look and feel of the website is, of course, important – they determine first impressions and build your brand – but it's also important not to get sidetracked by implementing design elements for their own sake.

Think about the purpose that a particular photo serves on your website. Consider whether certain embellishments could help your website perform its function better. Web design isn't all about function – an attractive and stylish website is great – but great aesthetics alone doesn't make a website perform; for that, you need to ensure that your design decisions and strategy are driven by the goals and purpose of the website.

The Importance Of Testing

Every website is different and serves a unique audience, so it's always best to fine-tune your strategy and tactics. Techniques that work well for one website may not work for another. How do you figure out what works best for you? You test. There are a couple of popular testing methodologies that will help you fine-tune your website: A/B testing (also known as split testing), and its more advanced sibling, multivariate testing.

A/B testing is the process of testing two variations of a page or items on a page against each other. For example, you might want to try two different calls to action to see which one works best. Each visitor gets a randomly chosen call to action, and your conversion goal for that visitor (e.g. whether they sign up) is tracked. After enough data is collected, the results show which call to action performed best.

Multivariate testing uses the same principle but allows for more variables to be tested at the same time. For example, you might want to test different versions of your website header, slogan, call to action or marketing blurb. Multivariate testing serves visitors random selections of each test item and tracks how well each combination of items performs.

While multivariate testing may sound fairly complex, there are tools available that make it really easy to do. One of the more popular tools is Google's Website Optimizer, which lets you perform A/B and multivariate testing on your websites. Best of all, the Website Optimizer is free, which means anyone can take advantage of these two optimization methods.

Knowing the theory and best practices is only one aspect of developing great websites that perform well. The second part is testing: discovering

Combinations	Page Sections					
Analysis for: Aug 21 2006 - Aug 21 2006						
View: ⦿ Best 23 Combinations ○ Worst 23 Combinations				Download: T ⬚ ⬚ | ⊕ Print | ⬚ Preview		
Combination	**Estimated Conversion Rate Range [?]**		**Chance to Beat Orig. [?]**	**Chance to Beat All [?]**	**Observed Improvement [?]**	**Conversions / Impressions [?]**
Original	31.2% ± 3.0%	├──▭──┤	—	0.41%	—	125 / 401
Combination 11	38.9% ± 3.1%	├────▭─┤	99.0%	85.4%	24.9%	160 / 411
Combination 4	33.6% ± 3.0%	├──▭──┤	76.8%	4.12%	7.74%	133 / 396
Combination 23	33.4% ± 2.8%	├──▭──┤	75.9%	2.82%	7.17%	153 / 458
Combination 16	32.7% ± 2.9%	├──▭──┤	67.8%	1.56%	4.75%	144 / 441
Combination 10	32.6% ± 2.9%	├──▭──┤	67.5%	1.69%	4.67%	139 / 426
Combination 8	32.4% ± 2.9%	├──▭──┤	64.6%	1.30%	3.90%	137 / 423
Combination 22	32.0% ± 3.0%	├──▭──┤	60.0%	1.03%	2.69%	129 / 403
Combination 7	31.6% ± 2.8%	├──▭──┤	55.1%	0.45%	1.27%	143 / 453
Combination 14	31.4% ± 2.8%	├──▭──┤	52.2%	0.41%	0.57%	137 / 437
Combination 21	31.1% ± 2.9%	├──▭──┤	49.1%	0.40%	-0.20%	126 / 405
Combination 18	30.3% ± 2.8%	├─▮──┤	39.1%	0.11%	-2.79%	130 / 429

Google's Website Optimizer.

what works and doesn't work and making adjustments. The Web isn't a fixed medium like paper, where changes are impossible. Your website is not in a finished state; it can evolve and adapt. So, to boost your conversion rates, you should test and optimize. ∎

Chris Spooner

How to
Turn a Site
into a

REMARKABLE
BRAND

The term "remarkable" means being worthy of notice or attention or, in the context of Web development, naturally persuading the viewer to mention or recommend a website to a friend. Developing a remarkable brand for your website means that people will likely give credit or refer to your website voluntarily, which is a big bonus when you are starting to build and develop your website.

Any niche or industry has hundreds or thousands of websites all based on the same topic, but from the crowd always emerges a bunch of websites that re-appear time and again. These websites are often mentioned in conversation and cited as sources of information or are the homes of highly sought after products. Given their high profiles, they can all be classified as remarkable, but how did they manage to build this great reputation?

This collection of tips and ideas is for anyone who runs their own website. While many of the examples given are from high-profile cases, the same techniques apply to any size website. Whether you're running a small personal blog or a large corporate website, the core methods behind each tip will help push your website to the top, make it more recognizable, help you be seen as an authority in your industry or niche, help you develop a successful community, increase traffic and sales and, most importantly, become a remarkable brand. Don't forget, implementing just one of these tips may give an extra boost to your website, but the combination of all of these techniques and a lot of time will give you the real results.

For example, a website that produces great content but has a mediocre design can certainly become a remarkable brand, and likewise a website that looks great but doesn't produce top-notch content on a regular basis can still be successful to a certain extent. Highlighting areas of weakness in these examples and taking steps to improve them could really benefit the performance of these websites.

Create A Unique Design

One of the first stages in developing any brand is creating a visual identity that represents the key values and ethics of the company, product or service.

This usually starts with the logo design, and continues on to promotional material and, of course, the website. In order to develop a remarkable brand, the design should be unique, stand out from the crowd and project a professional, trustworthy image worthy of a good reputation. A unique design allows a website to be recognized at a glance and not blend into the mass of mediocre designs out there. So, how do you go about designing a unique website?

Web Designer Wall earned a wealth of attention when it launched due to its attention-grabbing and inspiring website design, and it is still included in inspirational round-ups today.

Produce a design that is visually stunning

The Web Designer Wall blog has an intricate illustration that takes up a large portion of the website's background. The use of the large floral design, along with a range of well-designed elements and close attention to detail make the website unique and thus instantly recognizable and seen as a source of creativity.

Focus on universal design principles

The Black Estate Vineyard website has little color and no ornamental design elements, yet it is widely praised for its focus on a structured, grid-based design and excellent typography. The back-to-basics approach makes it stand out from the crowd of high-impact and over-the-top website designs, giving it a sophisticated and mature personality that fits perfectly with the topic of the website.

Black Estate Vineyard features an amazing design that follows key design principles, without unnecessary bells and whistles.

Create something that has never been seen before

The Silverback website gained huge exposure even when it was little more than a holding page containing an email sign-up area. The reason is that the website featured an amazing parallax effect that no one had previously seen in Web design. This single feature went on to receive a mass of attention and helped develop a remarkable brand for the Silverback application before it was even launched.

The parallax background illusion on the Silverback website drew a lot of attention for being so unusual.

Key Tips:

- Create a unique design that fits your industry or niche.
- Use your chosen brand identity across all online designs to consistently spread the same message and style.
- Pay close attention to details and produce a high-quality design.
- Don't jump on an already saturated bandwagon or trend.

Produce Interesting And Useful Content

The design of a website provides users with an immediate impression of the brand, but the content is what develops that brand over the long term. Content refers to the resources that a company uses to promote its product or service at a website and can include information published on the website itself, as in the case of a blog. Having truly remarkable content will ultimately develop the respectability of the brand. What can you do to develop exceptional content?

Provide useful information

ProBlogger constantly posts highly useful information on developing a successful blog, and readers learn and benefit from it. This content is then naturally passed around and recommended in social media. With consistently high-quality content, the website generates a remarkable brand as being a source of expertise.

Produce something people want to use

37Signals is the developer of a range of indispensible small-business and collaboration software. The high quality of the products has helped it develop a high-profile brand. Whether your website is for a product, company or service, the content has to be of exceptional quality for you to be able to build a following of people who will talk about and respect your content.

Become an expert in your field

By producing great online content with Wine Library, Gary Vaynerchuk has positioned himself as an expert in his field. This unique content has led

Darren Rowse of ProBlogger has developed a solid brand by consistently producing highly useful content.

to his being recognized as an authoritative figure, which has in turn developed the company and website into a remarkable brand.

Key Tips:

- Produce original content that solves a problem, gives advice or teaches something.
- Study the success of others and go one step further: get an idea of what "works" and then build on that concept.
- Be sincere in your aim to help people through your content.
- Don't make money your primary goal; otherwise the content of your website will lack in quality.
- Don't constantly promote yourself. Aim to help others and you'll get benefits in return.
- Don't give up; getting recognition through good content takes time and patience, especially in the early days.

37Signals offers a range of excellent software applications that have built a solid following of users.

Explore New Concepts

One of the best ways to stand out from the crowd is to do something completely different. Websites that use new media to explore unique ways of getting across their message can have a huge impact on their users. Video content is one tool that has recently allowed website owners to break free from traditional text-based interaction on the Web. Websites that use

Wine Library displays unique video content that conveys authority and expertise in the online wine industry.

video for informational or comedic purposes are seeing excellent growth and development of their brand. Let's take a look at some examples of how these new concepts can benefit a website.

Add your own unique twist

My Damn Channel is an entertainment studio that empowers comedians, musicians and filmmakers to create video series. The comedy series "You Suck at Photoshop" took the common screencast tutorial-style video and used it to present a hilarious series that follows the life of author Donnie Hoyle. The unique nature of the videos and the useful tips and techniques featured in them made them a highly successful viral phenomenon that, along with its other video ventures, earned My Damn Channel 12 Webby awards[1].

My Damn Channel released a 20-episode series covering various Photoshop tips and tricks, but with a very humorous twist.

Play off of popular culture

The Onion Network is a fictional news channel that posts up-to-the-minute video content based on current affairs and popular topics. Despite the realistic and seemingly serious nature of the videos, the content itself is a spoof. This creative content set a unique trend that helped it gain much popularity as a source of entertainment.

1   http://www.mydamnchannel.com/about.aspx

Provide entertainment related to popular topics

Diggnation is hosted by Kevin Rose and Alex Albrecht and covers the week's hottest tech and Web news through informal discussion. The relaxed setting of the show provides an interesting venue in which to deliver this information, and the informal chat and random conversation provides entertainment value. This personal twist sets the show apart from the surplus of other tech news websites, giving it a unique and remarkable brand that has gained huge exposure and a large fan base.

Key Tips:

- Explore concepts that haven't been done before on the Web, such as a TV-style series that tells a story.
- Look beyond the common format of blog posts to create unique content; video and audio provide many options.
- Add a personal twist to stand out from the competition.
- Play off of pop culture to develop a following in a specific niche.

The Onion Network consistently creates realistic news-broadcaststyle videos that play off of popular culture and current affairs.

Become Part Of The Community

Around any brand is a collection of people who form a community. These could be fans of the company, product or service or simply customers and users. The community is the most powerful asset any brand can have; these are the people who share their opinion or praise and freely spread word of your brand. However, they can just as easily call out errors and highlight negative aspects of your company, product or service if their expectations aren't met. In the modern world of communications, and with resources such as the Internet and social media, paying close attention to the community around your brand is a high priority. So, how are brands responding to their communities' needs?

Embrace social media and networking

Social bookmarking website Delicious monitors the Twitter search stream for problems, issues and comments about its service and responds with messages of help and advice. This method of directly assisting users creates

Diggnation discusses hot tech topics from the news website digg.com in an informal and relaxed setting.

a one-on-one relationship between the company and each user, making the user feel as though they have been heard and turning the user's experience into a positive view of the company.

Delicious uses Twitter to search for mentions of its service and strikes up conversations with individual users directly to help them with their problems and issues.

Appear friendly and approachable

Headscape is a progressive design firm based in London, UK. Along with its main stream of design projects, it has also developed a widely known web design podcast and a popular blog on which members of its staff (together with contributors across the globe) offer advice and tips from the industry. Showcasing the people behind the business gives insight into their personalities and provides a friendly connection. This positive feeling users get towards the people in the business is then naturally associated with the overall brand.

Be seen as a giver, not just a taker

Ryan Carson, founder of Carsonified, has seen huge success with his collection of high-profile Web apps. In an interview[2] he outlined some

2 http://boagworld.com/podcast/160-education-education-education

of his best tips for creating a successful Web app. One of these tips was to make it easy for staff to give credits of $5, $10 or $20 for the upcoming month, unasked. Likewise, if a customer experiences problems, an immediate refund of their last invoice instantly converts them into a happy customer. This idea of being seen as a giver, rather than simply taking a monthly charge, creates a sense of appreciation and positive attitude towards the brand. This generous approach creates a unique experience for the customer that binds them to the brand and encourages word-of-mouth advertising.

Key Tips:

- Create profiles for your company, product or service on various social networking websites and blogs to interact with your customers and users.
- Publish useful information through these streams to give users an incentive to join and become part of the network. Also, reciprocate any

Headscape supports interaction with its staff member Paul Boag through a podcast show, blog and individual Twitter profiles. This creates in users a friendly and approachable impression of the company.

friendships or Twitter follows with individual users to allow for a two-way connection.

- Give personal insight into the company, rather than simply using everything as a marketing tool.
- Be the first to help others with their problems with fast and efficient support, thus creating in them an overall positive attitude towards your brand.

Get Inside People's Heads

One of the age-old aims of branding is brand recognition, whereby a company, product or service becomes widely known in the marketplace. One benefit of this recognition is that you are instantly called to mind when people think of a certain topic. To become a remarkable brand, a website must get inside people's heads and subconsciously influence people's choices. It is also important to develop an initial strategy for how your brand is to be perceived. How do brands go about doing this?

Carsonified believes that freely giving to its customers is one of the most important habits when building a successful Web app.

PSD2HTML displays its banner advertisements on many websites and blogs within its niche.

Advertise everywhere

XHTML/CSS conversion company PSD2HTML understands the benefit of developing brand recognition. Its banner advertisements appear on a huge number of popular and high-profile blogs in its target niche. This constant recurrence of its brand name and identity creates a big chance that it will be the first company that springs to mind when someone is looking for an XHTML/CSS conversion company.

Be talked about

Andy Budd, of user experience firm Clear Left, appears in various interviews and gives many conference speeches on the topic of user experience in Web design. He also initiates a range of discussions through print publications, conferences and blog posts and Twitter activity. This gives him constant exposure and associates him and his company with his target niche, the result being that he becomes widely seen as an expert in his field.

Doing something memorable that is not necessarily directly related to promoting your company has its advantages in contributing to a good overall brand. Helping talented people in your field, supporting educational projects and running conferences to exchange ideas are all great examples of how a brand can be made remarkable through selfless acts.

Create viral or link-bait content

Common Craft received a mass of attention after publishing its first video, "RSS in Plain English[3]". Within a day, the video hit the front page of Digg and had been watched over 15,000 times. This kind of viral or link-bait content can really help generate a wealth of exposure and introduce your work to a whole new group of users. Overall, the extra attention gave the Common Craft brand a huge boost in becoming recognizable for its particular style of work.

The RSS in Plain English video from Common Craft became semi-viral content that received a mass of attention and links from various sources.

3 http://commoncraft.com/rss_plain_english

Key Tips:

- Advertise your company, product or service thoroughly within your niche. Aim to gain wide coverage rather than high click-through rates.
- Participate in discussions, interviews and topics to broaden your appearances across the Web.
- Create interesting and useful content that is likely to be passed around between friends and users in your industry.
- Be talked about. Ensure that your company, product or service has that extra special element that makes people comment.

Implementing these tips and techniques in the development of your own website will surely help build a respected brand. But don't forget that changes don't happen overnight. Building a remarkable brand takes constant and daily effort and attention. Be confident in your content, help others, spread the word and you'll be on your way to a remarkable high-profile brand of your own. ∎

Learning from
EXPERTS
interviews and insights

Steven Snell

M any of the most successful and well-recognized designers are willing and eager to provide guidance to others who want to improve their skills. We posed a series of questions to leading designers and developers in an effort to get some answers to common questions. The participants bring a great deal of diversity in skills and expertise, and all have valuable insight that can help those looking to grow[1].

Meet our panel of experts:

- Dan Rubin *(webgraph.com)*
  Founder and Principal, Webgraph and Co-Founder, Sidebar Creative.

- Jason Santa Maria (*jasonsantamaria.com*)
  Freelance Designer and Speaker.

- Paul Boag *(boagworld.com)*
  Co-Founder and Creative Director, Headscape; Founder, Boagworld.

- Jeff Croft *(blueflavor.com)*
  Designer, Blue Flavor

- Andy Budd *(clearleft.com)*
  Co-Founder and User Experience Director

- Collis Ta'eed *(envato.com)*
  CEO, Envato

- Wolfgang Barthelme *(bartelme.at)*
  Founder, Bartelme Design

- Keith Robinson *(blueflavor.com)*
  Principal and Creative Director, Blue Flavor

- Chris Spooner *(spoongraphics.co.uk, line25.com)*
  Freelance Designer and Blogger

- Jonathan Snook *(snook.ca, sidebarcreative.com)*
  Designer, Author and Speaker

---

1   Screenshots created with the browser Flock 2.5 under Windows Vista

- Tony Chester *(onwired.com)*
  Founder and Director of Operations, OnWired

- Elliot Jay Stocks *(elliotjaystocks.com)*
  Freelance Designer, Author and Speaker

- Khoi Vinh *(subtraction.com)*
  Design Director, New York Times

- Veerle Pieters *(duoh.com)*
  Graphic Designer, Blogger, and Founder of Duoh!

- Chris Coyier (css-tricks.com)
  Web Designer and Blogger, Chatman Design and CSS Tricks

- Jay Hilgert (bittbox.com)
  Designer and Blogger, Bittbox

- Dave Shea (mezzoblue.com)
  Freelance Designer and Founder of Bright Creative, CSS Zen Garden
  and Mezzoblue

- Darren Hoyt (darrenhoyt.com)
  Freelance Designer

- Henry Jones (webdesignledger.com)
  Freelance Designer and Blogger, Web Design Ledger

- Liam McKay (wefunction.com)
  Designer and Project Manager, Function

- Nathan Smith (fellowshiptech.com)
  User Experience Developer, Fellowship Technologies and Founder,
  SonSpring

- Nick La (ndesign-studio.com, webdesignerwall.com)
  Founder of N. Design Studio and Blogger

- Larissa Meek (agencynet.com)
  Associate Creative Director, AgencyNet

- Jon Hicks (hicksdesign.co.uk) Designer, Hicksdesign

Part I: Design and Development

What is one common myth or misunderstanding about Web design and development?

Dan Rubin: That it's something fundamentally different as a medium, and that solving problems for the Web requires radically different thinking than anything that's come before. This simply isn't true, especially where designers are concerned. The basic principles of visual design hold true when designing for the screen; the layers of interactive design, information architecture and other media-specific areas are just specialties related to the medium, just as architectural knowledge might relate to environmental graphic design, or as materials, printing and binding knowledge relates to packaging design, for example. The sooner a designer understands that, the faster they will become proficient in using the specific combinations of these layers that Web interface design requires.

Jay Hilgert: The most common misunderstanding I encounter has to do with the perception of clients. I'd say 90% of the clients I've dealt with underestimate the amount of work that making a website will be on their end. Paying a designer to make them a website isn't enough; the entire design depends on what content and message they wish to convey, and most of them don't realize how much thought they need to put into that. It's amazing to think that you can wait three weeks for a single paragraph of text from a client for their home page, but it happens regularly.

Wolfgang Bartelme: I guess the most common myth is that a certain design, and I'm speaking about Web design, can reach a point that it's finished. It's an ongoing process.

Keith Robinson: That mastering the tools (CSS, HTML, etc.) is all you have to do to be successful. I think one of the biggest problems young Web designers (and developers) have is a narrow focus on tools, as opposed to fully understanding the medium. I think knowing how to write HTML and CSS, as well as having a solid understanding of other technologies (Flash, JavaScript, etc.), is important, but it's equally important to develop non-technical or non-tool-related skills. It's good to know how CSS works, but

that doesn't substitute for understanding solid design and usability fundamentals, for example. As well, it's important to master interpersonal skills
and time management, etc. As an employer, I'd gladly take a lesser talent
if they're much easier to work with.

*What are common usability mistakes you frequently see from other designers?
What important aspects of usability are often forgotten but need to be considered when designing websites?*

Jonathan Snook: Probably the most common usability mistake I see designers make is making some things too subtle for the sake of aesthetics: links
or buttons that are not obvious or are hidden; things grouped too closely
together. The user should know what they're clicking on and why they're
clicking on it. Otherwise, they'll just ignore it.

Tony Chester: All too often, I see designers crank out websites with terrible
navigation. Yes, websites can be beautiful, but not at the expense of the
content. Yes, you can use a content management system, but not if it forces
you to have a stupid page flow. Navigation is critical, especially when the
main purpose of most websites is to sell something or share knowledge
or collect users' information. If users can't fulfill their goals on the website
easily, they'll leave, regardless of how the website looks.

Aside from that, I see too many designers trying to do cool things with Flash
and jQuery that simply make the website frustrating to use. I loathe dynamic menus that disappear too quickly if my mouse movement isn't precise enough. Give people big targets, and give them a little room for error.

*How do you feel about CSS frameworks? Do you think designers and deve-
lopers should use an existing framework, create their own or not use one
at all?*

Elliot Jay Stocks: I don't use any pre-existing CSS framework because I
prefer to work my own way rather than someone else's. So, I have my own
framework, which includes CSS, HTML and bits of PHP. I also make use of my
free WordPress theme "Starkers" as a starting point, so I guess you could
say that's a framework in some sense. In general, I think frameworks, especially your own, are a good idea because they speed up the build pro-

cess dramatically. If you do any task on a regular basis (which is inevitable, really), it pays to use a framework so that you don't have to keep repeating yourself.

Khoi Vinh: To be honest, I don't really care. If you are a passionate, ambitious designer or developer, it doesn't matter to me one bit whether you use a framework or not, so long as the end product is true to the spirit of the design and to the goals and needs of the people who will be using it. So long as you're not using Dreamweaver, it's okay by me.

Chris Coyier: If you are thinking of using a CSS framework because you don't understand how to accomplish the layout you are after, you shouldn't be using a CSS framework. CSS is a simple language. Writing it from scratch isn't so laborious that it necessitates some abstraction to make it more usable (e.g. the "on Rails" part of "Ruby on Rails").

That being said, CSS frameworks certainly have their use. Think of a grid-heavy, newspaper-style website. Every day, new layouts are needed to make things fit. The designers who maintain these websites need options and possibilities, not limitations. You can be sure that these types of web-

A creative menu
made with flash

sites are using frameworks to make it happen. They are using #home, .subColumn-3, div.first and .columnGroupB, semantics be damned.

If you are in this position, creating your own is certainly a possibility, but you would do well to check out some popular and time-proven frameworks before diving in. Blueprint, 960 and YUI grids, for starters.

Dave Shea: I see two main advantages to using frameworks: 1) less up-front work when coding a website, and 2) less cross-browser issues. In the case of the former, I've developed my own "framework" of sorts over the years that reduces the work when starting a new project. And in the case of the latter, I've gotten so familiar with Internet Explorer's quirks that I spend a lot less time debugging these days.

I've never cared enough to try one of the third-party frameworks like Blueprint, 960 or YUI. I figure that because I've been coding websites myself for ages, the time it would take me to hack one of them to my layout needs would be equal to or greater than the time it takes to just code it myself. Not to say they're not great for others. I'm sure they speed up development time for some people and help beginners ease into coding CSS layouts. But for me, frameworks are a non-issue.

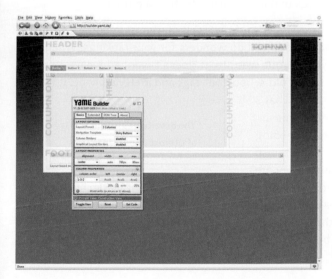

The YAML online grid generator works in a browser.

How would you describe the designer and developer's responsibility with search engine optimization?

Darren Hoyt: If you charge a competitive rate, you should already be building your websites with logical, semantic HTML that will complement the client's keyword-rich content, and ideally the CMS you're using should generate descriptive URLs. These things alone should be attractive to search engines. This shouldn't be an "extra" step; in my opinion, it should be standard.

As far as the developer's "responsibility" with optimization goes, it all depends on what is defined in the contract. Before a website goes live, I explain to the client that beyond writing good code, I cannot ensure for them stellar search engine rankings. I encourage them to think carefully about the content they upload and the people they exchange links with because it's the only thing that will bring them honest relevancy in the eyes of Google.

Personally, I would never define myself as an SEO expert to clients. I'd prefer to refer them to someone who has experience improving rankings. But I wouldn't refer anyone who relies on "baiting" Google in ways that are unethical or on methods that are plain ineffective or outdated.

Tony Chester: The developer's role in SEO is of utmost importance. Clean, standards-compliant code will do wonders for your rankings. When the Google bot arrives at your website, it doesn't want to weave its way through useless tables, old-school font tags and irrelevant code. It wants one thing: content. That's where developers come in. They are the key to feeding the bot with the content it so desperately desires. They are

> "The developer's role in SEO is of utmost importance".

the ones who write clean markup and create content hierarchy. They are the ones who make those pretty SEO-friendly URLs for you and create those XML sitemaps that Google loves so much. Without a well-built website, SEO is going to be a challenge.

Henry Jones: SEO can be broken down into two types: off-site and on-site. Off-site SEO is basically the number of incoming links to a website. Developers have little control over this. But on-site SEO involves using proper HTML markup, creating a solid website structure and making good use of internal links. Along with having a general understanding of how search engines work, developers should be responsible for all of these kinds of things.

Part II: The Design Process

What are your first steps when beginning a project for a client?

Darren Hoyt: In the project kick-off meeting, I try to set the tone by explaining why audience should be the #1 consideration. This immediately reduces the odds that the client will let personal aesthetic whims derail the design process. It also assures the client that I as a designer won't just be creating a portfolio piece for my own benefit. We'll both be working together to create an optimal experience for the user.

If the client hasn't considered his audience, we budget some hours for an "R&D" (Research and Development) phase in which we study the competition, make notes and wireframes and get an overall clearer profile of the type of users we're designing for.

Some other things to get consensus on during that kick-off meeting:

1. Ideally, the client should provide one point of contact, maximum. That person will understandably want to gather design feedback from co-workers and superiors, but allowing multiple people to call, email feedback and give conflicting opinions should be discouraged.

2. If a system like Basecamp will be used to track milestones, it's good to do an overview of the project schedule. Even if the dates change, it's a visual reminder to the client that we'll be working together to follow a formal schedule.

3. On that note, if there are going to be any vacations or gaps in the design schedule, they should be mentioned early on. I remind the client that

building a website is a two-way street that requires both of our ongoing availabilities. Sometimes this will scare a client off, but it's good to know up front if the client won't be holding down his end of the bargain.

4. To stay on budget, the mock-up process should be defined. Some clients will want to see three unique versions of the home page, while some will request a single home page mock-up and multiple internal mock-ups. Some projects depend on an estimated price, while some are a fixed price. It all depends on the project, but there shouldn't be any surprises.

5. Above all, content materials should be delivered before the mock-up phase. Remind the client that the website they are paying top dollar for will suffer greatly if the designer begins the mock-ups without all the right information. Design can quickly become mere decoration.

Jason Santa Maria: I always start by talking to the client about what they're trying to achieve and, if possible, talking to their customers or users. Every project starts out with research and discovery so that I can make informed decisions.

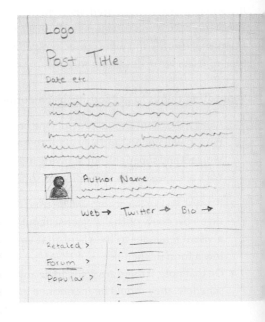

Chris Coyier: Defining goals is the ideal way to start. It's so tempting to jump right in and start designing stuff and laying stuff out. You can build a beautiful website jumping right in, but beautiful doesn't necessarily sell products or inform visitors or build community or accomplish whatever goals the client really wants to achieve.

The challenge is that clients may not be able to articulate what those goals are very well. As designers, as people with experience in building websites, we need to help them along in figuring out those goals. If you do this and then accomplish and exceed those goals, you will have some seriously happy clients.

What are some of the common challenges you encounter when transforming a rough sketch or prototype into an effective website, and how do you overcome them?

Liam McKay: For me, the biggest challenge is limiting what I do and focusing on what is needed. I don't struggle with having a lack of ideas; quite the opposite. Sometimes when I'm in the process of prototyping, my mind goes into overdrive, and I think of so many things to include that the design is in danger of being too overpowering. The hard part for me is working out which ideas are actually worthwhile and which ones are me just getting over-excited. The more projects I work on, the more obvious it becomes that working out what is really needed in the sketching process can help keep you focused and allow you to hold back a little on the things that might not be as necessary. That's not to say you can't try something new or different from the norm; it's more a case of building a solid foundation of essential elements and building on top of that.

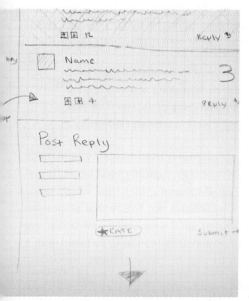

Mockups for a Smashing Magazine redesign.

Jason Santa Maria: The biggest thing I always struggle with is finding ways to bring the spontaneous and fluid nature of my sketches into the polished digital world. The best method I've found to combat this is to stay off the computer as long as possible. I keep sketching and honing my ideas, working in progressively more detailed stages and adding in new elements at each step, like color or more refined typography.

Nathan Smith: By far the most challenging aspect of a project is planning the information architecture. It is tempting to jump right in and start doing visual design or cranking out code, but if you do not have a good idea of what you are trying to build, then you will just be engaging in an exercise in futility.

To mitigate problems with ambiguity, I try to first approach the website layout by doing high-level wireframes. I like using OmniGraffle for wireframing. For larger projects, I will also do a taxonomy or mind map of all the categories of information that will go into the website. For mind maps, I like using a free tool called FreeMind. It allows me to quickly connect various nodes with other related topics. After a few minutes of shuffling things around, I usually have a solid grasp of the scope of the IA.

Once I know what I will be building and have a general page layout defined, then I delve into the actual interface design. For that, I have found no application that can rival Adobe Fireworks. It is by far the most versatile visual design tool in my arsenal. While others may prefer Photoshop, I am convinced that Fireworks is far better suited to the task of Web design.

"The most common challenge I experience is making a website cross-browser compatible (especially making it work in Internet Explorer 6)".

I generally tend to design on a grid. It is for this purpose that I have packaged my most commonly used templates and made them available for download at www.960.gs. Typically, I will begin throwing things around on either a 12- or 16-column grid, to see which ratios work for the content I am presenting. That is not to say that all designs should use a 960 grid, or even a grid at all; it simply gives me a starting point. It is easier to design with a few constraints than to be faced with a scary blank slate.

Chris Spooner: I find the main challenge of converting a sketch into a visual website design is creating and positioning elements with accuracy. The rough sketch does make the job of bringing together a full layout much quicker, but the lines and page elements aren't in proportion and therefore need to be recreated with accuracy and precision.

The main solution I use to overcome this problem is to base designs on an underlying grid, along with a bunch of margins and rulers in the software application. This helps me align the page elements to pixel perfection, which really brings the rough sketch to life as a solid and structured website design.

Nick La: The most common challenge I experience is making a website cross-browser compatible (especially making it work in Internet Explorer 6). To overcome this problem, I avoid using CSS properties that are not supported by IE6, or I use JavaScript.

Jay Hilgert: When designing a website, even in the earliest stages (in Photoshop), the number one thing I focus on is functionality; specifically, the user interface. I ask myself a series of questions like, "What is the most important information that needs to be readily available to the user?" This way, I don't get distracted by jumping right into the aesthetics, or the "faceplate" as I like to call it.

I establish an outline of content first, in order of importance, which helps me determine how and where to construct the navigation. (My goal is to have anyone who views the home page be able to know exactly what the website is all about less than a second after landing on the page.)

Once that's done, I start playing with the look and feel, doing my best to keep in line with the content, purpose and audience of the website. The challenges at this point are making it look good with as little load time as possible, optimizing the images, validating the markup, and getting rock-solid CSS. Testing and debugging are the final challenges, IE being the worst, as usual.

"Testing and debugging are the final challenges, IE being the worst, as usual".

How do I overcome these challenges? Lots of coffee, and music full blast.

How do you ensure that a website truly captures the essence of a business?

Jonathan Snook: This is hard because it's also about what a business wants its essence to be. Too often, it wants to be just like its competitors. It's important to understand the company. What are its core values? What market is it trying to attract? What is its current market? Take that information, combine it with any existing branding it may already have established and try to pull it all together. Remember that it's not about drop-shadows or the latest gimmicks. It's about creating something that is seamless and invites the user to complete whatever task they've set out to complete.

Larissa Meek: Know your objectives before you begin to design.

For example:
- What does the website need to do for the client?
- What does it need to do for the user?

An exemplary business website.

- What does the client want to push most?
- What will the user most likely do?

By having a good handle on both business objectives and user objectives, everything else should fall into place. The hardest part about design is that it is subjective, and everyone likes something different. So create something that you believe in, and be able to back up your design decisions with legitimate reasons. If you know the objectives and work towards meeting them, you will capture the essence of the business.

Nathan Smith: Before I even begin designing anything for a client, I always try to understand the two most important factors. First, who will be the users of the website? Secondly, what tone does the client wish to convey? It is my firm belief that by considering the target audience first and foremost, one can tailor the approach and even help guide the "voice" of the client as they formulate their approach.

As far as what tone to communicate, this depends largely on what makes the client unique. When working with ministries, I try to get a feel for the nuances of their theology and adapt my approach accordingly. For instance, some churches are purposefully edgy, while others are conservative.

Similarly, when working with non-profits, it is important to understand the purpose and vision behind the organization. You will probably want to feature case studies of the people whom they are helping.

When working with businesses, it is good to know who the competitors are and what their core products or services are, in order to highlight what differentiates your client from them.

Dave Shea: Understand the business. Some of my most successful work has been the result of talking to someone who plays a major role at the company and trying to understand their perspective of what the company does and who it serves. Once I get inside their head, it's easier for me to accept or reject design ideas that I think will or won't match that understanding.

Paul Boag: At Headscape, we have an entire methodology dedicated to capturing the essence of a business. This process sometimes involves mood boards and reference websites. Other times, it involves more abstract techniques. Two of my favorites are "design objectives" and "website personas."

Design objectives are similar to business objectives. With business objectives, you normally create a bulleted list of things that you want the website to achieve. With design objectives, your list includes messages and emotions you want to communicate.

Website personas have a lot in common with user personas. A user persona is essentially a fictional biography of a theoretical user that includes details about their lifestyle, job, education and other demographic information. A website persona follows a similar model but asks the question, "If your website was a person, what would that person be like?" Is your website a hip young teenager or a balding middle-aged businessman? These personas help define the essence of a website and give it a voice.

How do you determine which content management system is right for a particular project?

Darren Hoyt: Collaborating closely with the client during the initial project kick-off meeting and conducting a serious audit of their needs make the CMS decision a lot easier. I usually spend the first half of those meetings helping the client focus on big-picture issues like audience and message. In the second half, we work together to nail down a set of features that support the message. With a loose website structure in mind, we begin distinguishing between sections that need static page content and sections that require custom data types, like calendars, news archives and real estate listings.

When the meeting is over, we have a "recipe" of solutions to consider. For small and medium-sized businesses, WordPress plus a few key plug-ins can actually accomplish plenty. Especially in the last couple of years, the documentation has grown, the quantity and quality of the plug-ins have improved and clients love the control panel. Some open-source software takes a while to prove its staying power. At this point, WordPress has enough mainstream traction that clients actually ask for it by name.

"Some open-source software takes a while to prove its staying power".

Inside the WordPress engine.

If the client is very particular about the input and output of their data but is not comfortable touching any code, ExpressionEngine and Django are also great solutions that are endorsed by top developers. The learning curve can be steep compared to WordPress', but the level of control is much higher. Developers are able to create an admin environment tailored to the client's needs, which is invaluable if the client is especially high-maintenance. It's key to have a flexible control panel that can support any major changes the client may want a year or two down the line.

I also think it's good practice for developers to occasionally take the pulse of the community that surrounds a CMS. Are top developers endorsing it? Are the forums active? Is the documentation evolving? Are the plug-ins and extensions useful? Are upgrades happening regularly? Do the creators engage the public with status reports and plans for the future? Is public interest in the CMS growing or waning? Obviously, no one can predict the future, but if a CMS rapidly loses popularity and the support and documentation dwindle, it reflects better on you to have done your research and assured the client that he's getting another, more forward-thinking solution. Just as financial advisers get paid to follow public stocks, Web developers should be in the loop about software they recommend.

Paul Boag: There are two things I look at when selecting a CMS for a client: functionality and support. Most clients require the same core functionality (page creation and management). However, beyond that can be significant differences. You need to look at areas like search, permissions, workflow, asset management and customization. I also pay a lot of attention to the editor included in the CMS. This is what the client spends most of their time with, and many of them are terrible!

The second area you need to look at is support. You need to be sure that the CMS will be supported in the long term, so that the client can get the help they will require. Things to look at here are security (Are patches released regularly?), the development team, documentation, training and community.

Chris Coyier: The ideal answer to this question would be: I first evaluate the exact needs of the project, then test the strongest features of each major CMS against those needs and choose accordingly. Of course, it never works out that cleanly. Sometimes it's hard to know what the exact needs of a project are until you get further along. Sometimes the client already has ideas about what CMS they want to use. Sometimes legacy stuff is in place that affects your choice.

But most importantly, choosing a CMS isn't like choosing a new car. With a car, even if you've never been in it before, you still know how to drive it. You put the key in, turn it, shift into gear, press the gas, etc. CMS', perhaps unfortunately, are far more complex and share no such common bonds. So you can't just pick the "perfect" CMS off the lot and drive it home. There are significant learning curves with CMS' in learning how to use the back end, designing the front end and doing custom development.

What I actually do first is reach for WordPress. WordPress is the CMS I know best and has worked just fine for 80% of the client websites I've worked on. If I can make a website work with WordPress, I will; otherwise I'll look for something else. And I should say that this is not due to laziness. I've built websites in Drupal, ExpressionEngine, Sweetcron, Pinncale Cart, Magento and Cube Cart, and I've written a few CMS' myself. Reaching for what you know best saves time and sanity.

What is your approach to choosing a color scheme?

Collis Ta'eed: When selecting a color scheme for a design, my first stop is the logo and branding that I need to work with. I also like to look through any particular photos or other materials that I must use on the website, because it sometimes makes sense to match the color scheme to these items if they are going to be featured prominently.If nothing external dictates the color scheme, then I often stop by COLOURlovers[2] for palette inspiration because it gets me away from falling back on the same old color schemes.

Larissa Meek: Normally, I base a color scheme on a client's branding guidelines. However, if it is a new project, I find inspiration from books, magazines, illustrations and existing websites. Sometimes this is an organic process in which colors are discovered through design exploration, because textures and usability play a big part in interaction design.

I start with the home page and select a few primary and secondary accent colors that allow for contrast, which is one aspect of making a usable website. Once the overall look and feel is approved, I apply the color scheme to the rest of the website.

Elliot Jay Stocks: I'm not sure I really have a specific approach to choosing a color scheme. It depends on whether it has to tie into an existing brand, whether the client has identified a taste for a particular color or not and whether a certain atmosphere has to be evoked. If I'm stuck, I look around or visit color scheme websites like Kuler from Adobe.

Veerle Pieters: First I see if there is a style guide that defines the colors of the company. If not, I usually start with three colors if it is for a Web design: a dark and a light color and a bright color that contrasts well with the first two. The trick is to keep everything together in a harmonious way. Most of my color schemes, however, are chosen by intuition. They could be from an online source like Adobe Kuler or from a random picture that I extract colors from. In the past, I have also used colors from paint samples for interior design. There isn't a secret that I can share that works all the time, because I sometimes come up with a color scheme that seems like a good

2   http://colourlovers.com

match when seen in little square swatches, but when I apply it to the bigger canvas it really doesn't work. Experimentation is a big part of the process.

Jon Hicks: Being color-blind, I tend to rely on tried and tested schemes that I know work, or I take schemes from anywhere around me: posters, leaflets, photos, nature. Each scheme has a feeling and meaning, and the right one depends on the intended audience. For instance, for ReallyWorried.com's branding, calm and feminine colors were used (pinks and purples), whereas stimulating colors would have given an entirely wrong feel.

Adobe's Kuler requires Flash.

What universal principles of setting type do you follow in every project?

Jason Santa Maria: I just try to focus on the small stuff that's easy to overlook: legible type sizes, harmonious typeface pairings and proper punctuation.

Khoi Vinh: Only these: make it look good and readable.

Jeff Croft: Every project is different, so it's hard to say that I do any one thing for every project, but these certainly apply to 95% of the work that.

I do:

- Establish a baseline grid;
- Choose a "scale" of type sizes and stick to it;
- Limit myself to one, two or (very rarely) three typefaces;
- Establish appropriate leading and measure lengths;
- Use appropriate characters, such as proper quote marks and apostrophes;
- Be as subtle as possible while still being effective.

How do you know when a design is complete?

Wolfgang Bartelme: Ideally, a design is finished when you can't add or remove elements without making the design less usable or appealing. However, in real life, time and/or budget constraints tend to define when a design is done. And even if you declare a design as being "finished", new requirements will come up shortly and you will have to adjust or even rethink your design.

Collis Ta'eed: It's very difficult to know when to stop designing. Ideally I try to take a day or two off after I first have the feeling of being finished. Some time away from a design helps clear my mind so that I can look at it more objectively. More often than not, when I come back and look again I will see many, many flaws and start polishing the design by moving things around slightly, touching up details or even occasionally just starting all over again. The design is complete when I find that making changes actually makes things look worse rather than better.

Jon Hicks: You always reach a point with a design when you know you're just "tickling it." With one project, I took a step back for a day or so and then went back to it and started removing all the extra fluff, the tickles, reducing it to only the elements it needed. At that point, I knew it was ready: it had everything it needed to communicate, and no more. However, a design is never complete for me. I always look back on projects and see where they could have been more finished "if only I'd ..."

Nick La: To me, a design is never complete. Even after the website is launched, I often find ways to enhance it based on feedback.

Khoi Vinh: That's a great question. It's very hard to know when it's done. Of course, you look for a state when everything is balanced, in harmony, when every element has its place and behaves in a logical, consistent and yet still somewhat surprising manner. In another sense, too, a design solution for the Web is never really complete. It's just like a photograph, a snapshot in time, in which most of the elements are in place and orderly, but really what you're looking at is a moment in time, one state before the next state.

Keith Robinson: Is that a trick question? When it comes to the Web, a design is never really complete. It's pretty hard to tell when something is ready for the public eye, and

"It's pretty hard to tell when something is ready for the public eye, and I don't really try to dwell on it too much".

I don't really try to dwell on it too much. I always say that there is no such thing as "perfect" when it comes to design, and that's especially true on the Web. Go with your gut, launch your designs when you feel good about them and don't be afraid to make small changes once you're live.

Close attention to typography on a portfolio website.

Part III: Self-Improvement and Skill Development

Do you feel that designers and developers should have formal education and training rather than be self-taught?

Veerle Pieters: That really depends on the individual, but in most circumstances I would recommend a formal education to get a better understanding. Personally, I didn't have any education in the Web because it didn't exist back then. That part is self-taught, but I benefit a lot from the basics of design that I learned in school. I think concentrated education on design or development makes a significant difference, but continued education makes the most sense. Continuing education, post-formal training, is just as important. Because we're designing for the Internet, trends and technologies change. We need to adapt and grow. You aren't done once you are finished school; it is a continued process throughout your career.

Tony Chester: It depends. How good is the education? I've worked with some developers who have come out of school with incredibly strong back-

An (almost) perfect South Korean website for kids.

grounds. They have a fundamental knowledge of best practices that they can apply to whatever technology they happen to be working with. In those cases, the education is helpful. On the other hand, I've gotten resumes from recent Computer Science graduates who know Java and nothing else. They have the same foundational knowledge, but they can't seem to apply it to anything else. For those guys, the formal education isn't really helping.

The same thing goes for designers. If they can apply their knowledge of color theory and typography and layout to the Web – especially if their education was focused on print – they are in good shape. But I see far too many designers who can make something look pretty in Photoshop but have no understanding of navigation or usability or anything else that is necessary to creating a good website.

At the same time, plenty of people in the industry are purely self-taught and do some amazing work. For many of us, the Web was either in its infancy or didn't even exist when we were in school, so we've just learned on our own as things emerged. Ultimately, I think the best option is to have a strong formal foundation but also have the drive to keep learning and the ability to extend what you know to new media. The people who aren't limited by their tools will be the most successful.

> "We need to adapt and grow. You aren't done once you are finished school; it is a continued process throughout your career".

Andy Budd: It's great that so many people are self-taught because it goes to show how motivated and passionate people in this industry are. However, it does make it incredibly likely that they miss out on some of the fundamental building blocks of their chosen profession. For Web designers, this could be things like color theory, grid design and typography, all of which are lacking on the Web. It could also be more conceptual areas like design thinking and design criticism. Similarly, many developers are missing fundamental skills like software architecture, security, database planning and design patterns. So, while I think a lot of courses that focus on particular languages, software and techniques are a waste of time, these core skills are incredibly useful. Furthermore, as the industry matures, we're going to need people with increasingly specialized skills, such as design research, usability testing and interactive design. While these skills can be learned on the job, there are still too few agencies practicing them at an adequate level. As such, you're going to learn these skills at a much higher level if you enroll in a dedicated course.

Wolfgang Bartelme: Generally speaking, it's a good thing to have a formal education. However, that's just a starting point. You still need to teach yourself by attending seminars, reading books and, most importantly, just doing new stuff.

> "The people who aren't limited by their tools will be the most successful".

Collis Ta'eed: I don't believe it's essential to receive formal education or training; however, it is definitely one path, and there is certainly nothing wrong with taking that course. Personally, I taught myself for the most part and only enrolled in a night course so that I would have something to put on my resume. In the end, no one has ever asked me about my qualifications; instead, I have always been judged on my portfolio of work.

For aspiring designers looking to teach themselves, I can't recommend enough getting out some books on design fundamentals from the local library. There is a lot to be learned that can't (yet) be found online, particularly about the history of design and how it has evolved.

How do you personally meet the challenge of continual improvement and evolution as a designer?

Liam McKay: One way I strive to improve as a designer is by promising myself to try something new in each design. There was a stage before I launched my company Function when I was confident with my techniques but stuck in creating very similar designs. Everything had the same blue tint, and I used the same fonts, effects and style in each design. It led me to a point where I wasn't enjoying designing, and I knew I had to do something about it. So I decided that each design I did from that point on would include something completely new that I'd never done before. The other advantage of trying something new is that your portfolio becomes a lot more diverse. The variety of styles really strengthens your portfolio and makes you more desirable to potential clients.

I think it is safe to say that all designers are always pushing to improve their work and become better designers. The main thing that could get in the way is attitude: you should never feel that you are at the top of your game. There is always something new to learn, always something new to try. I'm very aware of the fact that I'm nowhere nearly as good a designer as I could be. And it's not something that gets me down; it just means that I've always got something to aim for and build on.

Dan Rubin: I'm always looking for new interests and creative endeavors that may or may not be directly related to design. I consider myself a "designer" in the most general sense; not a media-specific designer, but rather a

Konigi, one of many design showcases out there. This one focuses on user interface designs.

creative problem-solver in as many aspects of life as I find reason to apply myself. Challenging myself to constantly explore new things (e.g. photography, wayfinding and psychology), in addition to teaching and writing about these same interests, allows me to improve and evolve as a designer and as a person. Plus, it's way more fun than sticking to one thing. :)

Andy Budd: I don't believe the change is as rapid as people think. However, it gets complicated if you're trying to stay on top of twenty different fields. So, try to get really good at a couple of things and focus on those. That way, you'll always be ahead of the pack rather than continually playing catch-up. Blogs are obviously a great way to keep up to date on all the latest trends, but with so many to choose from, it can be overwhelming. This is why I recommend that people invest in their own professional development and attend conferences and workshops. Sure, you could learn it all from the Web given sufficient resources, but why bother when you can pick it up (and start charging for it) immediately for the cost of a couple of days of billable time.

Nathan Smith: Honestly, I try to avoid reading too many top-10 lists on design blogs. While those are helpful for finding tutorial articles on how to do various techniques with design software, there is very little to be gleaned in terms of design principles that stretch one's skill-set. I look elsewhere for inspiration.

Web design is still relatively new when compared to the rest of the disciplines in the "big D" design field. Therefore, I think the best way to learn about design is to look beyond our discipline. It is laziness that draws me to CSS galleries, looking at what others have done and imitating.

It has been said, "Art is meant to be appreciated. Design is meant to be used." While there has to be a certain level of aesthetics to design, I think that many of us in the Web design field often design to be admired. We want to win awards. We want our work to be on the front page of gallery websites, ranked with five stars. We want people to re-tweet our tutorials on Twitter. But really, to the end user, none of that matters. Great design is transparent. I am still learning to get out of the way.

To borrow a quote from Joseph Ballay of Maya Design, "It is in its transparency that it fulfills its function[3]".

Keith Robinson: Well, I'm constantly trying out new things and keeping my mind creatively engaged. It can be a real challenge when there is client work and the day-to-day business of being a working designer to do. I take time out of each day to sketch; or better yet, when I've got a personal design project, I work on that as much as I can. It takes discipline and effort, but it's those extra out-of-the-daily-norm moments that really help a designer grow.

> "Web design is still relatively new when compared to the rest of the disciplines in the 'big D' design field".

What separates a good designer from a great designer?

Dan Rubin: Understanding that design is not purely visual, and that visual or graphic design is only a small part of what we do as designers. When people ask me to define "design", I tell them that it's about creative problem-solving. The visual aspects are the result of executing the solution, whether you're designing a product, a Web application, a publication or a car. Knowing that your first role as a designer is "problem-solver", rather than "illustrator" or "guy who draws stuff" or even "Photoshop guru", means that your head's in the right place.

Paul Boag: Obsession, time and empathy. Great designers are obsessed with detail. They will spend hours making minor adjustments that will never be noticed but will add to the overall feel of the design. They also add elements that give a design that "Wow" factor. These embellishments won't be noticed by every user, but they will make the design memorable for those who do.

Of course, that obsession with detail takes time. I don't believe the majority of clients are willing to pay for great design, which is a shame. Sometimes it is up to the designer to put in the extra hours if they want to create something truly amazing.

3 http://maya.com/practices/human-centered-design

Finally, I think it is important that a designer is able to empathize. Ultimately, we are not designing for ourselves or our clients; we are designing for our end users. It is important that we really understand those users and relate to them on an emotional level. Good designers do usability testing, and great designers do that, too, but they also form an emotional connection with users that informs their designs.

Rate calculator at Freelanceswitch.

Jay Hilgert: If you ask me what separates a good designer from a great designer, it is the hunger to always learn more. In this industry, the stakes are constantly rising. The software is ever-evolving. A great designer is always hungry to learn more and to continue to get better, each and every day.

Nick La: A good designer follows trends. A great designer creates trends.

Part IV: Business and Freelancing

What tips do you have for designers on starting a business or small company? What should be done and what should be avoided?

Henry Jones: I have a couple of tips for designers who want to make it on their own. First, establish a high profile or, in other words, become well known in the design community. This may sound like a daunting task, but it can actually be quite easy if you have the proper skills. There are several ways to accomplish this, but probably the easiest is to have your portfolio and other projects featured on popular design galleries. This will lead to your work being seen by thousands of people each day, both fellow designers and potential clients. It is actually surprising just how many potential clients visit these websites in search of design talent. Once you have established a high profile, you will find that little to no effort is needed to find new projects, because they will find you.

Secondly, don't take on more than you can handle. Once those emails start rolling in with requests for your services, you will naturally want to say 'yes' to all of them, because establishing a good client base is important for a new design business. However, doing so can be detrimental to your reputation if you are unable to keep up and deliver high quality on all of your projects. A better approach is to only take on the projects that interest you and that are a good fit for your skill-set.

Liam McKay: When I went self-employed and started my blog and small design company I never really had a real plan. The only things I had were a lot of confidence and a solid understanding of good design. I saved a bit of money from old jobs and decided to dedicate some time to building my blog and some free resources to give away upon the launch of the blog. I was very conscious of the fact that a steady stream of traffic could bring a lot of potential clients, so the whole point behind the free icon set and free WordPress themes was purely to generate traffic, followers, friends and ultimately clients.

"The design community is definitely a very welcoming place; it's a community always searching for new information, resources, opinions and inspiration".

The design community is definitely a very welcoming place; it's a community always searching for new information, resources, opinions and inspiration. It's very easy to get involved, whether by making your own blog or website or by participating on other blogs. If you are looking to start your own blog or design company, it would be stupid to neglect the impact that involvement in the design and development community can have.

After working with my partner Spencer on building the blog and realizing how good he was at WordPress (and just how versatile WordPress is as a CMS), I decided that our best bet was to focus on our strengths: good design and solid WordPress development. Because of our focus on these areas, a lot of the work requests we got were based on WordPress, which made things a lot easier in terms of pricing, quotes and dealing with clients. People already knew what to expect: they knew what WordPress was, what it could do and what we could do for them. So without a doubt, associating ourselves with the two things we do best was a clever idea because it allowed us to focus on our strong points, and it meant that our clients were already very clued in to what we could do for them.

Jonathan Snook: One of the most important things to remember about running a design business is the business side. It's easy to get wrapped up in designing and client work, but you also need to be able to manage cash flow, taxes and sub-contracting, among other things. You also need to make sure you're charging enough for the work that you're doing. If you're used to a full-time job

> "One of the most important things to remember about running a design business is the business side".

that pays you $25 an hour, you may think that charging $35 an hour is worthwhile. Unfortunately, when you start tracking your time (and you should, even just a little bit), you'll realize just how little work you can reasonably get done in a day. That $35 an hour averaged over the course of a day starts looking like $10 an hour.

Chris Spooner: First, being confident in your skills and abilities is a great place to start before offering paid services. It's also a good idea to keep this in mind when taking on work, and not entering into projects that require coding languages and design styles that you're not completely familiar with. With this in mind, it's always useful to describe your specific skills or limit your work to a particular niche.

Keeping up to date in the industry is also crucial, especially with the world of Web design moving at an exceptionally fast rate. Being knowledgeable about upcoming changes, styles and new languages will keep you at the top of the game. Being an active blogger or social media user is a great way to constantly feed yourself and share this knowledge with fellow designers.

Andy Budd: The freelance market is extremely saturated, so to stand out from the crowd you need to be good at what you do and be able to prove it. This means developing a great portfolio of work for high-profile clients and then showcasing it in magazines, online galleries and events. It's very difficult to develop this quality of work by focusing on end clients, so I'd recommend working with agencies that can expose you to larger, more complicated projects. I recommend that both designers and developers specialize. For example, aim to be the best designer, front-end developer or Ruby developer in your particular area, and people will seek you out.

Jon Hicks: My biggest tip is, ignore your accounting at your peril. Make sure you keep money aside from each invoice for your tax bill, and ensure that all your paperwork is in order. If you have any doubts about keeping your own books, don't waste time with accounting software: hire a bookkeeper and accountant. If you compare the cost of them doing it to you doing it at your hourly rate (and possibly getting it wrong), which would you rather do? They'll also be able to advise you on running your business and how to save on your tax bill.

"Keeping up to date in the industry is crucial, especially with the world of Web design moving at an exceptionally fast rate".

What main principles should you follow in designing a portfolio website?

Larissa Meek: Showcase your best work and not all of your work. Case studies are a great way to highlight the strategy behind your design choices.

- List technology and software you have used.
- If you have a diverse portfolio, live filters for sorting projects can be helpful (e.g. filtering by Flash, CSS/HTML and mobile projects).
- If it's a personal portfolio, list your role on each project.

Elliot Jay Stocks: Provide links as well as images (in fact, any portfolio that just shows images without any links that people can follow to verify the work is, in my opinion, a bad and potentially unreliable one). Let the work shine, and allow the content to breathe. Be honest about what you did or didn't do on a project. Wow the visitor by showing them the breadth of your work, but at the same time don't bog them down with too much content. Include a minimal amount of written content with each portfolio piece, unless it's a specific case study. Keep case studies to a minimum: five is enough, and any more won't get read.

Veerle Pieters: First of all, the work should do the talking, because it is your calling card. If you are a Web designer, you should use W3C guidelines as best practice. Take care of the little details that show the labor of love, such as thinking about typography. Don't use a completely Flash-based website, but use Flash in a well thought out way. Don't make things overly complicated by over-innovating. Put yourself in the mind of potential clients and think of how many steps are needed to get a picture of the work. Don't be afraid to show your work at a big size, so that potential clients really see the details without having to squint at tiny images. Be honest about what your part was in a job. All too often, I see examples of people who aren't clear about their part in the process so that clients will believe they

The portfolio of Shannon Moeller from Colorado, US.

did it all. This doesn't help you in the long run. There isn't anything wrong with specializing. You don't have to be a one-stop shop to be successful.

Chris Spooner: Because a portfolio website is a showcase of a designer's skills and knowledge, I think the main principles are to present a good understanding and knowledge of design theory by putting them into practice

Gregory Wood impresses the visitors of his blog with unconventional layout; every blog post has its own, unique design.

with the actual design of the portfolio itself. However, I also believe that the overall portfolio design shouldn't be so brash and in your face that it takes away from the examples of your work; so, I'd say a slightly minimalist design that focuses on layout and typography is a good style to aim for.

An insightful "About" page is also a handy addition to any portfolio. It's a great way to introduce yourself to prospective clients and allows for that interaction between your personality and the users.   ■

Behind
the
Curtains:
The Smashing Magazine Story

How did Smashing Magazine come into existence? How do we work, and what happens behind the scenes? What is our secret recipe for success? Our readers are asking, and Smashing Magazine is answering.

The Smashing Magazine story is not the classic story of two guys coming up with a great idea in the right place at the right time. It is a story of dedication, patience and hard work ... **truly** hard work. During a conference that Vitaly attended recently, he was asked by an energetic young fellow about the secret formula of Smashing Magazine's success. Trying to be honest and open-minded, Vitaly did his best to explain that there was no such thing, that it's only a matter of being *truly* passionate and engaged in the work that you do. Vitaly pointed out the necessity of working hard, better than others, and, most importantly, never giving up if you strongly believe you are doing the right thing. After a couple of additional questions intended to glean more concrete and quantifiable insights, the young fellow abruptly walked off and faded into the crowd, probably feeling he had not been taken seriously.

The simple truth is that Smashing Magazine does not have a unique formula for success. We have certain goals and a certain understanding of how to achieve those goals, but the most important quality along the way has been a strong willingness to live up to the expectations of the design community, despite the time and money that requires. There is no clever, shrouded strategy behind it, and no puppet-master deciding which articles best fit this or that advertising campaign. Smashing Magazine is and always has been independent. The quality of each article is measured purely by the extent of its utility to our readers. We respect our readers and protect their interests. This is the main principle of our work, and we work hard to make sure that this principle is never compromised.

How It All Started

Perhaps the most unusual thing about Smashing Magazine's birth is that we never actually sat down together to discuss the whole thing. We never threw up a whiteboard and brainstormed on a groundbreaking concept for a successful magazine with a solid marketing model. In fact, Smashing Magazine is the result of a random experiment, initiated by two like-minded Web workers with shared passion and knowledge, as well as valuable experience (Sven) and energetic motivation (Vitaly).

It all started in August 2006. Vitaly Friedman, a computer science student and freelance Web designer with 8 years of experience, had been occasionally writing articles for the legendary German online magazine "Dr. Web[1]". The magazine had been known on the German-speaking Web design scene for over 12 years. The man behind the magazine's curtains was former freelance designer Sven Lennartz, who had managed to make editing and maintaining Dr. Web his full-time job.

They both had obligations of their own to address: Vitaly doing freelance gigs and passing university exams in Saarbruecken (in south-western Germany), and Sven keeping up with Web design developments, discussing article ideas with authors and coming up with innovative ideas for Dr. Web from Luebeck (in northern Germany).

At this point, we had known each other for over two years but had never actually spoken by phone or met in person. Casual discussions about recent developments and ideas for new posts took place via the convenience of email[2]. It is no surprise, then, that the idea for a big collaborative project was modestly suggested via one of these numerous emails. To be honest, it wasn't really a big deal for either of us. It was Sven, actually, who came up with the idea for an English-speaking online magazine for designers and developers; and once Vitaly suggested the name "Smashing" ("We smash you with the information that makes your life easier."), we both decided to give the idea a try by setting up a basic blog, publishing a couple of posts and just seeing how it went. We had neither financial support nor any signed agreements at that point.

> The quality of each article is measured purely by the extent of its utility to our readers.

---

1 http://drweb.de
2 Things aren't much different now, either. Most of the time, we discuss articles and the development of the magazine via email or occasional Skype calls. Big changes are usually discussed in person in various cities across Germany.

All big and small details of the project, including back-end, front-end and publishing considerations, were discussed via dozens of emails. accompanied by loud speaker systems and sketched notes, which is probably why most of those emails had interminable subject lines ("Re: Re: Re [34]") and also why we needed so many emails to agree about *anything*. Interestingly enough, all of the building blocks of the new project were put together by Sven and Vitaly separately, in German pubs and local pizza places, during long walks and between (or during) university lectures.

After two weeks of preparation, the domain was registered, the server configured and WordPress installed. We adapted one of the first minimalistic WordPress themes we found, and there it was, ready to be used. The Smashing Magazine website went online on the 8th of September 2006. The magazine didn't even have a logo then: we used the default Verdana headline from the WordPress template. The first articles were taken from Dr. Web, translated from German to English and then published on the newly born Smashing Magazine.

The first articles weren't a huge success, of course, but we didn't expect success either. We didn't celebrate or conceive any big plans. We carried on with our own things, remaining patient and determined. Several months passed, in fact, before we achieved our first significant breakthrough.

How We Got To Where We Are

Things progressed slowly; after all, we both had our own things to take care of. Initially, we agreed to publish two articles per week at most, using the content from Dr. Web as a baseline and producing new content on top of it; for example, we expanded the German articles and refined them for an international audience. Traffic grew gradually over the first couple of months, but we didn't observe significant spikes in traffic until the end of 2006, when our stories (those early "list" posts) started hitting the mighty Digg's front page[3].

---

3 Yes, you can blame us for all the design-related lists that have floated onto the Web over the last few years. We didn't invent the format, but we took it to a more sophisticated, usable level.

The first time our eyebrows raised was in response to the huge traffic jam caused by the article "50 Beautiful CSS-Based Web Designs in 2006", which landed on Digg's front page and gained over 3100 votes. Our server crashed a couple of minutes after that Digg effect, of course; after all, the images were over 150 KB each, and the dedicated server wasn't exactly configured for this kind of traffic spike. A couple of weeks later, "53 CSS Techniques You Couldn't Live Without" literally smashed us with over 5300 Digg votes. That was the turning point in Smashing Magazine's development: from then on, our stories did pretty well in social media, delivering traffic and interest in ad spots. At that point, we knew we had to rethink our modest plans for the magazine. We also knew we had to finally meet each other... for the first time.

It wasn't our idea to earn a living with this online magazine. We had no pressure to succeed, and we could afford to be patient and move the magazine in the right direction at its own pace. Experience in and passion for Web design helped us avoid errors and allowed us to keep doing our own thing. Once we realized that the design community was interested in our posts, we went further and made posts longer and better structured. We also included more images and illustrations; some readers complained (and

Drafts of the Smashing Magazine logo, up to April 2007.

still complain) that the length of our posts repeatedly slowed down their RSS feed readers and machines. Undeterred, we continued smashing our readers with huge posts. Some of these posts were so huge that they could easily be used for a standalone website, which is why we started offering our posts in PDF for easy printing.

Of course, lengthier articles meant more work and more commitment from us to our little project. We scoured the Web for wallpapers, tools, CSS and JavaScript techniques, tutorials and other resources; we tracked and presented design trends and common usability problems; we also re-

Illustrations from all of Smashing Magazine's articles. The detail shown here is part of a collage of over 650 images.

searched advanced topics, such as data visualization, and interviewed designers and experts to gain more professional insight. By this point, we had developed a set of tools to help us automate the process of collecting useful resources and preparing design showcases. We could now publish more articles per week. With Tuesdays and Thursdays already reserved for huge posts, we decided to provide our readers with image-heavy inspirational posts through a regular "Monday Inspiration" series.

And, of course, more images meant an even bigger server load. To keep up with the growing appetite of our visitors, we had to regularly expand our server farm. Readers often discovered us through social media websites: we certainly could not have gained so many without Digg, StumbleUpon and Delicious. Because our articles were useful or inspirational, they were often bookmarked and recommended, which leveraged the power of social media to spread the word and bring us traffic. Frederick Townes, Neil Patel, Muhammad Saleem, Victor Battera, Dave (BlueNile), Tal Siach and other friends helped us better understand how social media works and how important these media have become on the Web.

By the middle of 2007, we were finally starting to run out of Dr. Web articles. By then, we were already publishing a mix of translated articles and original content: Vitaly wrote articles from scratch, while Sven wrote new articles in German that Vitaly translated into English. Smashing Magazine's readers were quickly getting used to our trademark lengthy posts. Most Dr. Web articles didn't fit this new style: they were much shorter, and some focused less on Web design but rather on project management, SEO and the marketing side of Web development. So, we gradually switched to producing original content specifically for Smashing Magazine.

We quickly found, though, that our command of the English language wasn't as good as we had thought. More and more, our readers complained about grammatical flaws, spelling mistakes and unclear sentences. So, we started looking for a professional proofreader. Unfortunately, it took over a year until we finally got in touch with the right one, Andrew Lobo, who has been doing a great job editing most of Smashing Magazine's articles (and also this book) since November 2008.

Our publishing frequency grew, as did our readers' expectations. Late in 2007, we realized our audience had grown significantly, resulting in an extremely diversified readership. Meeting the expectations of these readers with only two to three articles per week was becoming harder. This was the time when we started engaging regular writers.

Sean Hodge and Mark Bloomfield were the first guest writers to help Smashing Magazine widen its horizon with new topics and formats. With them, we could publish four to five articles per week. Once those first guest posts were published, we started receiving inquiries from designers and developers across the globe. It turned out to be a good arrangement, because freelance writing is usually an intermittent thing that many designers can do between projects. When a new project comes along, the writers can just drop writing if they don't have time for it.

And so we were permanently looking for new writers. It wasn't an easy search, and it took us a long time to find authors who would write for us regularly. We looked passively (responding to email inquiries) and actively (searching for bloggers who have a deep understanding of design, usability and coding). We even organized a Smashing Author contest, in which our readers could send us guest posts; we published the most interesting ones, and the author of the best post (as selected by readers) was awarded an Apple MacBook Air. The prize (and its delivery) is a story of its own, because R. Christie, the writer of the winning post, "Top 10 CSS Table Designs", lives in Indonesia.

Ironically, we never really found regular writers through the contest itself, but we did manage to attract the attention of many freelance writers across the globe. Within a couple of months, we had engaged a couple of excellent regular writers, such as Steven Snell and Jacob Gube. Later, other authors (Vailancio Rodrigues, Jean-Baptiste Jung, Chris Coyier, Kayla Knight, Inayaili de Leon, Noura Yehia, Aquil Akhter, Danny Outlaw, Cameron Chapman, Glen Stansberry and Matt Cronin) were writing for us. Our active searching led us to Chris Spooner and Dmitry Fadeyev, who are also contributing authors of this book. These new authors not only infused the magazine with innovative ideas but brought new life to it, too, making it possible for us to cover areas that neither of us are particularly knowledgeable in and freeing up our time so that we could write articles about topics that lie closer to our hearts.

But by covering topics that were new to us, we ran into the challenge of having to maintain the high quality of our publication, because we simply didn't know if the write-ups we were getting were actually correct and incorporated the best design and coding practices. So in late 2008, we started asking professional designers and coders to consult on and edit some of our articles. For instance, PHP gurus Chris Shiflett and Sean Coates noticed some major mistakes in one of our articles on PHP, and we asked them to write a rebuttal. When it was published, we used the occasion to publicly apologize for our mistake and any inconvenience caused by it. Since then, we have approached unknown subjects rather carefully, trying to consult professionals before putting the articles online.

Smashing Magazine's 2nd Anniversary Poster, created by James White in August 2008

By 2008, our publishing schedule had accelerated to five to ten articles per week. (We used to take weekends off, but even that changed eventually.) Since then, we've received regular inquiries about writing positions and never missed a chance to try one out and see how it works. Between late 2007 and 2009, we had published articles by over 120 writers from all continents of the world. Unfortunately, we haven't met any of them in person, but hopefully we'll change that in future.

Of course, in addition to the Smashing Author contest, we have run other contests to give our readers an opportunity to participate and produce their own smashing content. In collaboration with our readers, we have released header graphics, textures, typographic templates and <hr /> lines as free downloads. As you would expect, the winners of these contests were awarded some very cool prizes. Probably the most famous contest we've run is for desktop wallpaper calendars, in which designers across the globe send us their wallpapers every month, and we publish them before the

The Desktop wallpaper calendar series is one of

beginning of the following month. Vitaly suggested the idea for the contest to Sven, who was skeptical at first. In fact, we intended to keep it going for only 12 months, but our readers wanted more, so of course we couldn't stop. Sometimes we do giveaways just for their own sake. We've really enjoyed smashing our readers with useful prizes over the years. A couple of years ago, we never would have imagined that we would be giving away so many high-quality freebies down the road. Some of the giveaways are not commissioned by us but rather contributed by designers; in turn, we do our part to deliver huge traffic and great publicity to them. It's a pretty good deal, in fact, particularly if the freebies are well designed – what you would call a win-win situation at its best (for both the designer and publisher). Elena Gafita's WordPress themes and Jos Buivenga's free fonts were the first freebies we released. Since then, we have released over 130 high-quality freebies from over 100 designers across the globe, and we are genuinely grateful for all the hard work that designers and developers put into them and for making them freely available to the community.

the most successful series on Smashing Magazine.

Of course, we have also encountered difficulties along the way. Over the course of three years, Smashing Magazine received over 44,000 emails and sent out over 17,000 replies (which averages to about 40 incoming and 15 outgoing emails per day). Because we were the only two processing these emails, we had to prioritize. So we made an effort to answer the most important emails immediately (otherwise they would wind up in the long queue beckoning for our attention), but many emails weren't replied to in time (or at all). We tried to go through each and every email we received, but sometimes that was impossible. Meanwhile, we experienced three serious mail database crashes (thankfully, we had back-ups) and lost data from two over-heated disk drives. Because of this, a couple of nearly completed articles were never published: unfortunately, they never made it to our WordPress engine.

Another difficulty we encountered was the growing traffic of our magazine. In December 2007, after two Digg effects, a Reddit effect, a StumbleUpon effect and a huge Slashdot effect, all in a row, our darling Web host throttled our server for a couple of days and eventually threw us out. Apparently, the load was so high that the server gave up the ghost. We never found out exactly what had happened or why we were shut down. Apparently, our little blog caused significant performance problems on the server (even back then), drew too much traffic (we had a flat rate for traffic till then) and wasn't profitable for the host. Not everyone knows that a project like Smashing Magazine can't be hosted on a typical Web space or managed server. We needed more. Much more. And apparently dozens of terabytes of traffic are quite costly.

> A project like Smashing Magazine can't be hosted on a typical Web space or managed server.

Our Web host wasn't the only one that didn't like us, though. For a while, Google didn't like us either. We had been selling text links without the "no follow" attribute and were subsequently banned from the Google index in 2007. We removed the text links immediately, and a couple of months later we were back in the index.

Currently, our monthly traffic hovers around double digits in terabytes, and we have a customized server whose main base is in Germany, not far from where Vitaly lives. We have six servers permanently running to deliver images and content to our readers. The servers were configured and are permanently maintained and optimized by Rene Schmidt, who is also a contributing author of this book. He also takes care of the customized WordPress plug-ins being used on our root server to serve millions of page impressions per week.

As we write this chapter, Smashing Magazine contains 761 articles overall, plus a couple of pages. That's not a lot, but those 761 articles have generated over 130,000 comments and trackbacks. Many of those comments we got in February 2009 during our hardware giveaway: we wanted as many comments for that post as possible, and we got them. At 8999 comments, WordPress crashed.

Key Ingredients Of Our "Success" Story

Although a new-born idea can take probably dozens of routes to becoming a success story, one thing is clear: success requires a hell of a lot of hard work (no big revelation, but worth pointing out nevertheless). Although some of our readers have claimed otherwise, we have always avoided convenient shortcuts that would have gained us more exposure from less thorough work (also known as "filler content"). Sometimes we deliberately chose the difficult path if it meant gaining exclusive, valuable content (for instance, when we prepared surveys and case studies that each took up to as many as 60 hours of work, a record we have found tough to beat).

The look of Smashing Magazine was never as important as the quality of its published content, either to us or our readers.

Indeed, **valuable content** – or, more precisely, the process of writing, editing and publishing valuable content – has been the most important aspect of our work over the years. Content is certainly king, and in our case it turned out to be a real silver bullet. The truth is that Smashing Magazine has never had a breathtaking or visually appealing design: our headings used to be ridiculously large, our search engine wasn't exactly killer for years and some design elements were inconsistently aligned and styled.

But none of that really mattered much. The look was never as important as the quality of its published content, either to us or our readers. While completely ignoring the visual design, we invested instead in usability, functionality and, most importantly, valuable and relevant content. This content is what has driven visitors back to our website over and over again.

One lesson we learned early on was the importance of saying 'no' to the enticing offers that inevitably spring up from all around. The moment you get the hang of whatever it is you are doing, you are immediately surrounded by dozens of sharks wanting a piece of your success and grabbing your attention with compelling offers. Actually, these sharks don't even really know what they want from you, aside from a piece of your success and any "partnership" that would boost traffic to their own websites or put money in their pockets. From the very beginning, we decided to remain consistent and do our own thing – and do it properly. Avoiding distractions up front helped us prevent problems down the road.

Our famous RSS-feed icons, designed by Dirceu Veiga from Brazil and released by Smashing Magazine for free in 2008.

If we had to identify the principle that has had the biggest influence on our work over these years, it certainly would be that we've gone to tremendous lengths to understand our audience and live up to its expectations. We continually listen to what our regular readers ask and complain about in the magazine, and we also monitor the conversations that take place beyond our magazine; for instance, in blogs, forums and social media. We continually analyze and prioritize the information that crosses our path, following up on what is potentially useful and discarding what would not benefit our readers. Evidently, though, when your large (and particularly diverse) audience has built up high expectations, failing to meet those expectations becomes very easy. Readers always seem to remember those controversial articles that were really torn apart in the comments; references to those articles always pop up in the comments section, usually beside phrases like "Worst post ever."

So to find the right direction for the magazine, understanding the needs and interests of our audience became particularly important. One of the simplest ways to gain this insight was to put ourselves in the shoes of our readers[4]. This was quite easy, in our case. Being Web developers ourselves, we decided to focus on content with the highest utility, as judged according to our own expertise. It turns out that thousands of designers across the globe have interests similar to ours, and our expertise has apparently been good enough for them. From the very beginning, this criterion of utility has been the sacred premise of our work; it has defined and continues to define the nature of the content we publish.

Our readers often ask how we manage to read their minds: i.e. publish an in-depth article at the very moment they are looking for resources on that topic. We aim to deliver content that is useful and usable, so it's no wonder that we publish articles the same day that some designers and developers start looking for them. Bottom line: we found our audience, and our readers have found a magazine that has helped them in their daily work. In the end, it has worked out simply because we had (and still have) a good understanding of what our readers need.

For this reason we decided to try out Twitter in August 2008 (which was actually very late). We were aware of various life-streaming applications and wanted to try one out and see how it worked. To be honest, we were skeptical at first but eventually got used to it. We experimented with the service, trying to figure out how we could use it to better communi-

---

4 Of course, understanding one's audience is not absolutely a golden rule for all success. For instance, many artists take a rather more self-absorbed route and simply do whatever they want, utterly neglecting public opinion. In our case understanding the needs of designers was vital, or else we wouldn't have been able to reach that audience at all.

cate with our readers. In the end, we came up with various ideas that are all intended to more tightly integrate readers into Smashing Magazine's daily routine.

We now share useful pointers on Twitter, as well as (hopefully) innovative ideas and personal insights behind the scenes. We also invite our Twitter followers to actively participate in the decision-making process. For instance, our followers can decide which articles are published next and suggest interesting ideas for future posts. We also follow up on our readers' dilemmas and questions in the "Ask SM" section of the magazine. Twitter has become our main communication channel with our audience and has allowed us to learn more about our readers, get them involved and better anticipate their needs and interests.

What Happens Behind The Scenes?

At Smashing Magazine, quality control has always played an enormous role, probably taking up over 50% of the time of preparing posts. We see it as our job to advocate for the readers' interests and to make sure that our published articles are correct, useful and well presented. This last point explains why most posts take over 20 hours to prepare, correct, edit, revise, update and re-edit again and again, as often as it takes to come up with truly smashing results.

Posts take such a long time to prepare also because they are usually the combined work of a large group of people spread across the globe. We often work with additional contributors from Russia, Australia, Asia and South America to ensure a diversity of voices and uniqueness of content. We also try to incorporate the feedback of our Twitter followers. The editorial team thoroughly reviews each submission and then, if it accepts it, revises and adds to the original article.

Good is often not good enough, and our authors often notice as much from the numerous changes, additions and (hopefully) improvements introduced by the editorial team, even after they have submitted what may be a fifth version of an article. There is no "optimal" number of articles that we aim to publish each day, and we don't care how prominent the author of an article is: our goal is to deliver high-quality content.

Unfortunately, our judgment occasionally misleads us, and we do make mistakes, whether by asking an author the wrong question or providing readers with the wrong answer. But we are aware of the responsibility that we carry for every single word and image that we publish. We gladly

smashing magazine
we smash you with the information which will make your life easier. really.

(X)HTML template systems in PHP »
// october 1st, 2006

Web developers find themselves sooner or later in a dire situation: their scripts become an entangled mess of code. Program logic, presentation logic and in a worst case scenario even layout and design are so interconnected with each other that the further development becomes difficult. Would one have thought ahead and had created a clear structure for the code - the so-called HTML-template-engines, the integrity of the layers would have been preserved.

A HTML-template-engine serves to separate program logic (PHP) from layout, (HTML) and design (CSS). Most existing template-Systems are not limited to HTML-models. They are generally usable for E-Mail and even XML.

Program code can be changed independently of the web site design. All this is theory though. In practice and complex projects this division can not be realized most of the time. To prevent inflating the program code unnecessarily with representation logic, another fourth level is often added. In this layer logical connections are processed, which directly affect the representation. Example: Table line paging or dynamic lists.

A further substantial advantage of HTML templates is the reusability of program code, design and layout. A template can be used in numerous places on a web site. Changes in a template affect all pages where this template is being used. This can save a considerable amount of time and money, because instead of several pages, just the template has to be changed and proofed.

Levels

Program logic
On this level typical script tasks are settled, for example retrieval and conversion of data from the data-base. If the HTML template system is initiated, variable html templates are assigned to the appropriate substitute symbols.

Layout-level
It consists of models, for example of HTML. The model of a specific site can be composed of several templates, which are joined in program logic more directly by the template system. The layout too will partly be determined on this level;

pages

Home
About

categories

Color palettes » (2)
Lists » (5)
Tips a (1)
Trends » (1)
Tutorials (1)

News-Feed

Previous Posts

- HTML Template Systems
- List of Best SEO-Tools
- Color Palettes: Insurance
- The List Of Lists
- Color Palettes: Traveling
- Symbols, Buttons & Icons
- Web 2.0 Design Trends
- List of CSS Tools
- Nifty Tools & Diagrams
- 1 User Online

Smashing Magazine in its early days. This is how our design looked like back in October 2006.

Some of the icons released by Smashing Magazine between 2008 and 2009.

welcome every bit of constructive criticism, and all feedback helps us become wiser and stronger and avoid similar mistakes in future. We also continually review our guidelines for quality, improving and reworking them whenever necessary. We learn from our mistakes and are honest enough to admit and apologize for them, and we strive to get it right the next time, which is an important part of our philosophy.

What may look like a rigid, demanding workflow is actually quite a creative and productive environment. In our experience, the initial communication with an author is critical to getting a great article, so we always encourage writers to ask questions and share their problems with us. We often suggest interesting points and directions to take that may not have occurred to the author.

It is important to us that our contributors feel comfortable with the topics they write about and are excited by the content. To avoid any misunderstandings during the writing process, we give authors a set of templates and a style guide outlining our requirements and expectations.

In turn, we do not restrict an author's creativity with deadlines. It's up to the author to decide how much time she or he needs for an article and how much effort to put into it. We know enough to appreciate great effort and dedication, which is why time-consuming, high-quality articles are often rewarded with generous payment bonuses. One of the core principles of our work is to treat our writers fairly. We never hesitate to reward authors for their good work;

for instance, by paying them a tidy bonus for finishing their 10th article for Smashing Magazine. We spend a sizable amount of money on our writers, and we know they deserve every cent they get.

We also pay attention to quality content that our readers are interested in. Permanently useful articles and resources are bookmarked locally and globally, tagged and evaluated (some articles are prepared over several months, with a new tool or technique added to each one every day). It takes time to see connections between topics, determine the best format for an article, write it all down and pass it along to the writer, or write it ourselves. When browsing Web designs (either sent to us or found online), for instance, we pay attention to the smallest details, such as the design of the comment form, the placement of buttons, typography, layout and the alignment of design elements. We store them all in a library of original and creative ideas that later form the foundation of new posts.

One thing is clear: filtering the huge amount of information we both receive via RSS and Twitter is time-consuming, but investing a manageable 30 to 60 minutes every day pays off. Discovering new feeds is essential, and removing irrelevant ones is necessary, too. Many ask us how we find new content using the same sources. Well, we don't use the same sources. We talk to people, we use Twitter, we use a number of international sources (Vitaly can read and write in English, German, Russian and Polish) and our international contributors help as well.

Thank You, Web Design Community

Around the middle of 2008, we received a lengthy email from a graphic design teacher in South Africa, who complained about the lack of educational materials in his area. He told us that every evening for a couple of months, he would select an article from Smashing Magazine and prepare it to be discussed in detail with his students. It was one of his ways of teaching the main principles of good graphic design. Aside from a couple of old library books, Smashing Magazine was his only resource for the course. His simple reason for writing was to express his and his students' sincere gratitude to the design community for its tremendous support, its freely available articles and its outstanding engagement and readiness to help. This remarkable email got us thinking: the community hasn't always been this way. With the rise of design-related blogs and magazines, you are never alone today as a designer; someone is always there to help you. As designers, developers, publishers and readers, we should all recognize that the design community has passed a significant milestone in its development. We may not have noticed it, but we have all done a great job of connecting ourselves, sharing our passion and spreading the word about best design practices and useful tools and resources.

Perhaps the most incredible yet overlooked characteristic of the design community is its friendly, enthusiastic spirit. Every day now, literally thousands of talented, hard-working folks out there gain new insights from their work, come up with brilliant ideas and then share their experience with fellows designers. Nourished by the gratitude of its benefactors and powered by the reach of social networking, the design community has produced an enormous variety of high-quality articles, resources and tools, available to everybody. Every single contribution supports the whole community, and the community supports these contributors via traffic and word-of-mouth advertising – the networking effect at its best.

The truth is that Smashing Magazine could not exist without these contributions. The most important element of the magazine is and always has been our readers. And the magazine could not have become what it is today without the strong support and engagement of our authors, hundreds of contributors and the millions of people who have visited and recommended our magazine since its launch. Our job is not only to contribute to the design community but to help maintain this fertile environment in which ideas are born, insights are exchanged and discussions take place, making the lives of designers and developers easier and richer. You are the ones who set the wheels in motion and made it all possible. Every contribution, even the smallest, made a big difference. And we want you to know that we recognize that and that we respect you and appreciate your support. We'll do our very best to stay true to that in future. ∎

The Authors of the book - page 1

	Alessandro Cattaneo	Andrew Maier	Chris Spooner	Darius A. Monsef	David Leggett	Dmitry Fadeyev
Age	31	23	24	28	20	24
Pets*	4	2	2	3	1	2
Computers	4	1	2	4	3	4
Displays	4	1	2	3	1	2
Browsers	4	7	7	3	5	5
Cell Phones	2	1	1	2	1	1
Working Hours	40	35	30	60	60	30
Vacation days	28	20	1	30	0	14
Books**	1000	200	2	100+	15	81
Aliases	8	2	2	4–5	1	1
Shoe size	9½	12½	9	12	10	9½
Countries visited	14	3	4	13	10	9
Words***	4.161	4.107	2.443	2.021	4.107	4.593

The Authors of the book - page 2

	Jacob Gube	Jon Tan	Kayla Knight	Rene Schmidt	Steven Snell	Sven Lennartz	Vitaly Friedman
Age	26	35	20	33	30	47	24
Pets*	2	1	2	1	2	8	4
Computers	3	2	2	5	3	6	3
Displays	1	1	3	5	4	5	1
Browsers	4	Lots	2	11	6	4	6
Cell Phones	1	1	1	1	1	1	1
Working Hours	55	-	20	50–60	60	50	60
Vacation days	14	-		5	25	6	?
Books**	122	?	12	20	100	104	80
Aliases	0	1	1	1	1	0	3
Shoe size	10½	8½	8½	8½	11	10	13½
Countries visited	12	21	2	8	7	15	9
Words***	3.075	4.161	3.075	4.888	9.443	2.680	2.680

*   Pets (including input devices)
** Books you have at home and in the office
*** Amount of words/symbols your article has

Index

www.smashingmagazine.com

facebook.com/smashmag

twitter.com/smashingmag

http://www.smashingmagazine.com/
the-smashing-newsletter

www.smashingbook.com